THE HARRISON BOOK OF KNOTS

THE HARRISON BOOK
OF KNOTS

BY

P. P. O. HARRISON, *Master Mariner*

Original Drawings by the Author

GLASGOW
BROWN, SON & FERGUSON, LTD., NAUTICAL PUBLISHERS
4-10 DARNLEY STREET

First Edition   -   1964
Second Edition   -   1972
Third Edition   -   1978
Reprinted   -   1993

ISBN 0 85174 346 3
ISBN 0 85174 095 2 (Second Edition)

©1993—BROWN, SON & FERGUSON, LTD., GLASGOW, G41 2SD
Printed and Made in Great Britain

PREFACE

In these days when so many beautiful things are mass produced it may seem a waste of energy to labour at a handicraft: but it should be borne in mind that a craftsman made the original article, and that without his skill, the machines would have nothing new to produce.

The life of the sailor of old was singularly adapted to the development of the handicraft of Fancy Ropework. The reason that he so occupied himself is on account of two major factors: his inability to read and the availability of the material. The art of Fancy Ropework reached the peak of its excellence about the middle of the last century when a slump in trade brought about a reduction in the number of crew in a ship with the consequent reduction of the spare time that had permitted sailors to occupy themselves with their handicraft. An observer at that time considered that in the way of knots, especially for use at sea, there could be nothing more to invent. He was wrong. Much more has been invented since then. Probably more than existed at that time; and the writer himself has some novel contributions to the craft to offer in this book. Given a piece of string man will find some new way of tying a knot with it.

The Manufacturer has encroached on the decorative art of the sailor: machine made Sword-matting has largely replaced the Coachwhipping that used to cover Companion rails, although so far there is no substitute for the Turk's-Heads that conceal its rough ends. The famous Ocean Plat Mat once invariably graced the head of an Accommodation Ladder, but seldom does today. A manufactured one has taken its place. But the Bellrope seems to have escaped the attention of the manufacturer, which is surprising when one considers how many bells there are and how simple it would be to make a plastic Bellrope of great artistry. Until the day that this happens sailors will still have to make their own: and in the making of Bellropes there is an immense field for ingenious activity.

A sailor, or any other person, who was absorbed in such a hobby would never find time hanging on his hands: for not only do ships' bells require

iii

Bellropes but the bells of schools, churches, and many other places where a bell is a necessary part of the equipment.

Recently the writer sought 'sanctuary' during a blizzard in Rochester Cathedral where he was refreshed and entertained by the staff and clergy. The beautiful gleaming bells that had once belonged to H.M.S. *Kent* badly needed their Bellropes renewing, and the writer's offer to do this was gladly accepted. Later when visiting the Cathedral he was informed that one of the Bellropes had been stolen and a further replacement was made. The Canon remarked that it would be interesting to meet such a passionate admirer of fine ropework that he would steal from a Cathedral. The compliments of both the Canon and the thief were much appreciated by the writer!

It seems to the writer that there must be a world shortage of Bellropes. In his endeavour to forestall the Manufacturer he has made them for schools, churches, ships, yachts, homes, a seminary, a cathedral, a shipyard, several 'pubs', and a number for his shipmates. He verily believes that had he accepted payment he could have done better than he has at sailorizing!

It cannot be claimed that this book covers the whole field of knotting that could be employed in the making of Bellropes: but it covers a great deal, and some of it has never before been seen in print. What is explained will be sufficient to enable the reader to grace a bell with a beautiful Bellrope. It is suggested that he acquires some rope and the few simple instruments that are necessary and sets to work. He will be surprised how time flies, and he will be well rewarded with the result of his efforts.

At Sea. *February*, 1963.

CONTENTS

SECTION I

HOW TO MAKE SHIPS' BELLROPES

SECTION II

AN INVESTIGATION INTO THE OCCURRENCE IN GENERAL KNOTTING OF CERTAIN BASIC KNOTS

SECTION III

BASKET MAKING

SECTION IV

MISCELLANEOUS KNOTS

SECTION I

HOW TO MAKE SHIPS' BELLROPES

CHAPTER I

THE INSTRUMENTS

THE making of Bellropes requires very few instruments. A used razor blade and a meat skewer would be all that was needed for the making of the Continuous-cord Bellrope. With the addition of a large darning needle any bellrope described in this book could be made. But tools for the purpose are available and it would be preferable to have them rather than raid the kitchen and the workbasket.

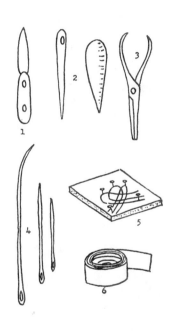

No. 1. *A knife.* It is better to get a good one that will take an edge.

No. 2. *A marlingspike or wooden fid.* The marlingspike is steel and must be kept free from rust otherwise the ropework will become stained. The fid is of boxwood.

No. 3. *Pliers.* The long-billed type are the most suitable as they may be inserted between strands to nip and pull through a strand. They are also useful for pulling needles through rope.

No. 4. *Needles.* A large Packing needle is easily threaded and is useful for reeving cords when making Standing Turk's-Head No. 24. Sewing needles of several sizes are useful; but a good darning needle will do the job almost as well.

1

No. 5. *A cork mat and pins.* The easiest way to make the Crowns for the Fancy Turk's-Heads is to place a tracing of the Crown on a Cork mat and pin the cord along the lines of the tracing. A stiff cushion would make a suitable substitute for a Cork Mat. Ordinary household pins are suitable for the purpose.

No. 6. *Adhesive tape.* This is used extensively. It makes a good Parcelling (No. 52). When making Continuous-cord and Wall-and-Crown Bellropes always seal the ends of the cords with adhesive tape to prevent them fraying.

You will need a pencil and some tracing paper for transferring the designs of Crowns from the book to the Cork mat, or for working out your own designs. In this case a rubber will also be needed. Any over-and-under design can be developed to form a Turk's-Head. Flatten out a Common Turk's-Head (No. 22) and it will be seen that it makes an attractive mat.

CHAPTER II

BASIC KNOTS

Three simple basic knots, all allied, are used extensively in the making of Bellropes: The Wall, The Crown, and The Diamond.

No. 7. *The Wall Knot.* Open the strands in a rope and turn them down against the stem. Take each strand in turn and tuck it upwards and under the next strand to the right. This is a Right Wall Knot. Tied in reverse it is a Left Wall Knot. In nautical parlance the knot is referred to simply as a Wall.

No. 8. *The Crown Knot.* Open the strands in a rope and hold or seize them upwards from the stem. Take each strand in turn and tuck it downwards and under the next strand to the right. This is a Right Crown Knot. Tied in reverse it is a Left Crown Knot. It is generally referred to as a Crown, the word Knot being dropped.

No. 9. *The Diamond Knot.* Open the strands in a rope and hold or seize them against the stem. Take each strand in turn and pass it upwards to the right over the adjacent strand and under the next strand. This is a Right Diamond Knot. Tied in reverse it is a Left Diamond Knot.

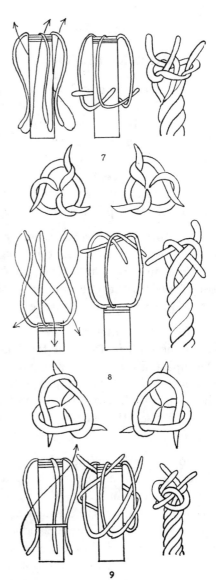

3

CHAPTER III

THE CONSTRICTOR KNOT

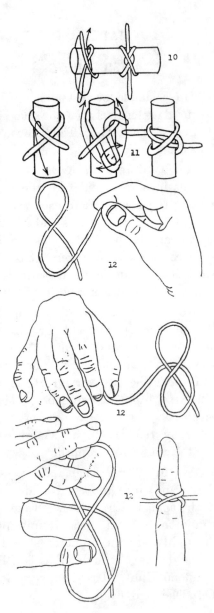

As the Constrictor Knot is so often needed in the making of Bellropes a Chapter has been given to its construction. It is undoubtedly the greatest Binding Knot. As a tourniquet it is unsurpassed except that it is only loosened with difficulty, often only with the aid of a sharp instrument.

No. 10. *The Direct Method.* Follow the sequence shown in the diagram. The knot may be made on the finger and transferred to the Bellrope, or it can be made directly on the Bellrope itself.

No. 11. *Another Direct Method.* Cross the cord in front on the finger or Bellrope and grasp the outer end. Draw it below and under the inner end. Give the loop a half twist to the right and place it over the end of the finger or Bellrope.

No. 12. *The One Hand Method.* Take the cord in the right hand and form an ampersand (&). Without letting go of the cord, pass the end behind the upper loop of the ampersand. With the forefinger and thumb press the two loops together. This method of making the Constrictor Knot, and the method

4

that follows were invented by the writer. It occasionally happens that one hand is engaged, as when grasping a handful of cords in the preparation of Spanish Hitching (No. 59). It is then that the One Hand Method of tying the knot is useful.

No. 13. *Another 'Trick' Method.* Take a piece of cord with two hands. Form a loop with the part held in the right hand behind that held in the left hand; and hold both parts in the left hand. Figures *A* and *B*.

Figure *C*. Hold the bight of the loop in the right hand and draw it from behind the hanging end. Twist it in a half circle to the left and bring the loop thus formed over the loop in the left hand. Pass a finger through both loops and draw both ends taut. Figure *D* shows the completed knot.

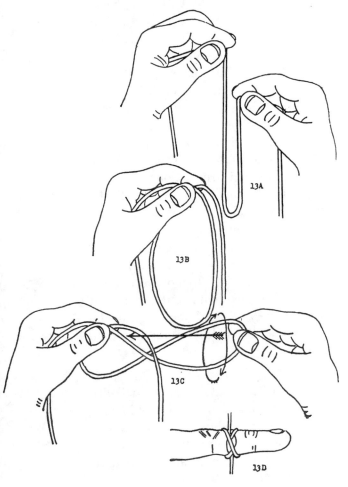

CHAPTER IV

MULTI-STRAND BELLROPE KNOTS

No. 14. *The Matthew Walker Knot*. This attractive knot, especially if followed by a Star Knot (No. 15), makes a handsome decoration on a Continuous-cord Bellrope. Turn back the strands and seize them to the stem. (Figure *A*). Twist the strands to the right to form a 45° helix. (Figure *B*). Take each strand in turn and pass it spirally to the right under the next and all the other strands and bring it out under its own part. (Figure *A*). When all the strands are tucked secure a piece of paper round the work with adhesive tape. Remove the seizing. Grasp the paper and take up some of the slack of each strand in turn. Remove the paper and draw all strands up taut. The knot may require a little 'moulding' before the strands lie snugly alongside each other.

No. 15. *The Star Knot*. This is the most decorative and complicated Multi-strand Bellrope Knot, and the making of it is a considerable achievement. Star Knots are generally made with a minimum of five strands and a maximum of eight. Grasp the stem in the left hand. Commence by forming a Half Hitch with each strand and passing the

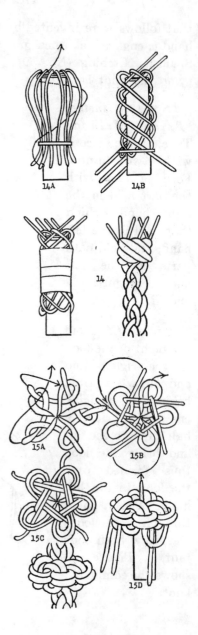

6

end of the strand through the loop of the next Half Hitch to the right. Work the Half Hitches up snugly to the centre (Figure *A*.)

Form a Left-hand Crown with all the strands. Figure *B* shows the completed Left-hand Crown. Tuck each strand back above the loop of the Half Hitch and under its own part. With each strand in turn follow the lead inside the adjoining strand to the right, over one Half Hitch, and down through the loop of the next Half Hitch. Figure *C* shows the knot at this stage, and Figure *D* shows another view of it. Continue to follow the lead underneath the knot and tuck each strand in turn up through the centre. (Figure *D*). Each stage is simple in itself and once mastered may be made in less than five minutes.

No. 16. *A Diamond Sennit Knot.* This is a variant of the Diamond Knot (No. 9). Turn the strands down and hold or seize them to the stem. Take each strand in turn and pass it to the right upward and outside all the other strands and tuck it through its own part. Take in the slack of each strand a little at a time until all lie snugly. In appearance this knot is similar to the Matthew Walker Knot (No. 14) except that the strands emerge from the rim instead of the centre. This knot is used when finishing a Round or Square Sennit.

No. 17. *A Diamond Sennit Knot.* This is also a variant of the Diamond Knot (No. 9).

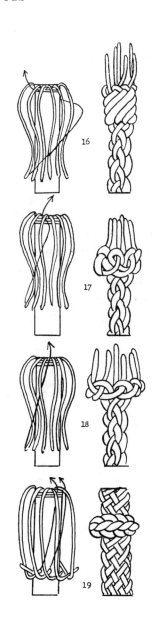

Turn the strands down and hold or seize them to the stem. Take each strand in turn and pass it to the right upwards and over the next two strands and tuck it back under the second one. Draw all the strands up snugly. This knot is used for finishing Round or Square Sennit.

No. 18. *A Diamond Sennit Knot.* This is a variant of the Diamond Knot (No. 9). Turn the strands down and hold or seize them to the stem. Take each strand in turn and pass it to the right upwards over one strand and under one strand. Draw up all the strands snugly. This knot is used for finishing Round and Square Sennits when making Continuous-cord Bellropes.

No. 19. *A Diamond Sennit Knot.* This variation of the Diamond Knot (No. 9) gives a half-round effect and is a very attractive knot. Turn the strands down and Wall them to the right (See No. 7). Take each strand in turn and pass it to the right upwards over one strand and under one strand. Draw up all the strands snugly. This knot may be used to divide Round Sennit from Square Sennit when making Continuous-cord Bellropes. (See Chapter VIII).

CHAPTER V

TURK'S-HEADS

Sailors have employed much time and patience in the evolvement of complicated Single-cord Turk's-Heads: but as the same effect can be obtained by the more simple Built-up Turk's-Head (No. 27), the writer has been able to reduce the Single-cord Turk's-Heads to two basic types from which two others are evolved. The nomenclature used to describe these Turk's-Heads is original.

No. 20. *The Simple Turk's-Head.* This knot is sometimes tied in hand and then transferred to the Bellrope; or it may be tied directly on the Bellrope. Follow the illustration carefully. If tied in hand, when the two ends meet (Figure 20B) transfer the knot to the Bellrope. The lead may then be followed as many times as necessary. This is generally not more than three. To make the knot more secure apply a dab of glue before cutting the ends which should then be concealed. Turk's-Heads may be made more attractive by outlining each side of the cord with coloured thread. The Simple Turk's-Head forms the basis of the next, and more complicated, form.

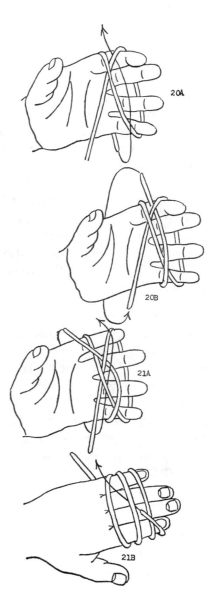

9

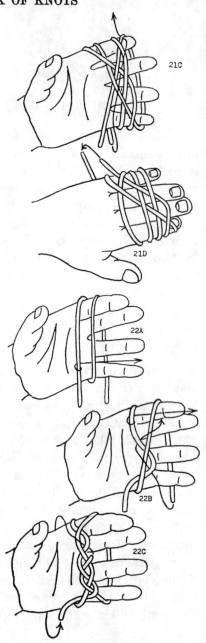

No. 21. *The Compound Turk's-Head.* This is an extension of the Simple Turk's-Head. On reaching the stage illustrated in Figure No. 20*B*, continue winding the cord round the hand following illustrations 21*A* and 21*B* carefully. It will be seen in these illustrations that in one instance the cord passes over two parts before being tucked. Illustrations 21*C* and 21*D* show the final under-and-over sequence of the knot.

No. 22. *The Common Turk's-Head.* This is the only other Single-cord basic Turk's-Head that it is necessary to know. It is the Turk's-Head most commonly used on board ships and hence the name. If it is examined carefully it will be seen that it is simply ordinary three-strand platting. Follow the instructions given in illustrations 22*A*, 22*B* and 22*C*.

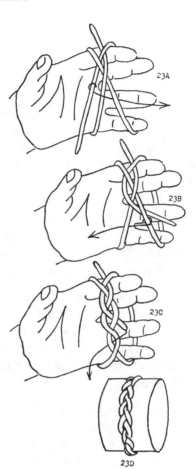

No. 23. *The Narrow Turk's-Head.*
This is also an extension of the Simple
Turk's-Head. On reaching the position
shown in illustration No. 20B, make an
ordinary plat of the three parts. This
is shown in illustrations 23A, 23B and
23C. This is an ideal knot for use on
Bellropes with large girths. The knot
may be easily extended. With the above
four knots all that is necessary for
decorating Bellropes with Single-cord
Turk's-Heads can be accomplished.

The next series are known as *Standing Turk's-Heads*; the strands or cords with which they are constructed being attached to the Bellrope itself. They may be strands that are being 'cut out' when reducing the number of strands in a sennit; or they may have been reeved through the Bellrope.

Standing Turk's-Heads may be made of two, four or up to eight strands.

No. 24. A single cord reeved through the rope will make two strands (Figure 24A). Follow the illustrations given in Figures 24B and 24C, and follow the original lead two or three times as desired.

No. 25. *The Crown and Wall Turk's-Head.* The bight of the cord if reeved through the rope and then cut will give four strands. Crown the four strands to the right as in Figure 25B, then Wall them to the right as in Figure 25C. By following the original lead two or three times a handsome Turk's-Head is achieved.

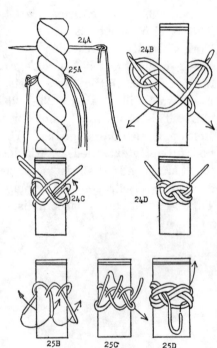

No. 26. *The Long Footrope Knot.*
This gives an altogether wider knot than
the Crown and Wall Turk's-Head. It
usually consists of at least six strands.
Form a Right-hand Diamond Knot
(Figures 26*A* and 26*B*). Upend the work
and form a Left-hand Diamond Knot
below the first Diamond Knot. (Figures 26*C* and 26*D*). Follow the original
lead two or three times.

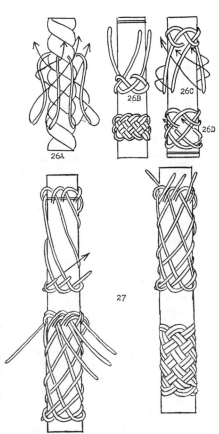

No. 27. *The Built-up Turk's-Head.*
Using the method described here, a
Turk's-Head of any length can be made.
Either reeve a number of cords through
the rope or secure them to the stem
with a Constrictor Knot. (No. 10).
Crown all the cords to the right and
wind them round the rope in a right-
hand spiral. At the base of the spiral
Wall all the cords to the right spiralling
them upwards over-and-under and follow
round the original Crowning. The first
lead may be followed as many times as
required. Usually three is sufficient.

No. 28. *Coachwhipping*. This work, as the name implies, is also used in the making of leather whips. Prepare four narrow strips of duck canvas or other suitable material. Fold the edges in and iron them flat. To get a spiralling effect two of the strips must be of a contrasting colour to the other two. Arrange the four strips as in Figure 28*A*. Pass the upper left-hand strip round the back of the work, between the two right-hand strips, and lay it below the remaining left-hand strip. Now pass the upper right-hand strip round the back of the work, between the two left-hand strips, and lay it below the remaining right-hand strip. (Figure 28*C*). The rough ends are concealed in the illustration with Simple Turk's-Heads. (Figure 28*D*).

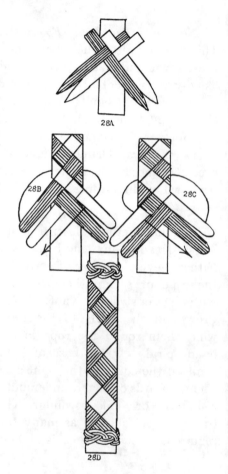

No. 29. *Coachwhipping* with a diamond pattern. Prepare four strips of
duck canvas or other suitable material.
Paint them with contrasting colours or
use   differently   coloured   material.
Arrange them as in Figure 29*A*. Pass
the upper left-hand strip round the back
of the work, between the two right-hand
strips, and lay it below the remaining
left-hand strip. Now pass the upper
right-hand strip round the back of the
work, between the two left-hand strips,
and lay it below the remaining right-
hand strip. (Figure 29*C*) Conceal the
rough ends beneath Simple Turk's-
Heads (Figure 29*D*).

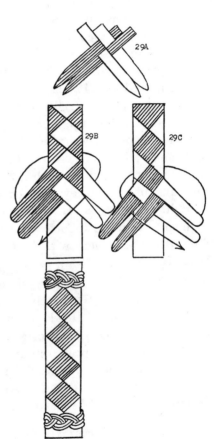

No. 30. *Six Strand Coachwhipping.*
Prepare six strips of duck canvas or
other suitable material. Fold in the
edges and iron them flat. Arrange the
strips as in Figure 30*A*. Secure them to
the stem of the Bellrope with a Constrictor Knot (No. 10). With three
strips in each hand take the upper left-
hand strip and pass it behind the work,
under-over-under the right-hand strips
and place it below the remaining two
left-hand strips. Then take the upper
right-hand strip and pass it behind the
work, under-over-under the left-hand
strips and place it below the remaining
two right-hand strips. Having made the
rough ends secure with Constrictor Knots
(No. 10) conceal them with Single-cord
Turk's-Heads.

The knots that are now described
are the Fancy or Decorative Turk's-
Heads. The Turk's-Heads that come
under this heading are all original and
have never before appeared in any work
on knots; but the 'mats' and 'crowns'
from which the Turk's-Heads have been
developed are already well known.

No. 31. *Single-cord Half-loop Decorative Turk's-Head.* The original 'mat'
from which this Decorative Turk's-
Head was developed was shown the
writer by the Chairman of his Company,
Mr. F. E. Harmer, who had seen it in a

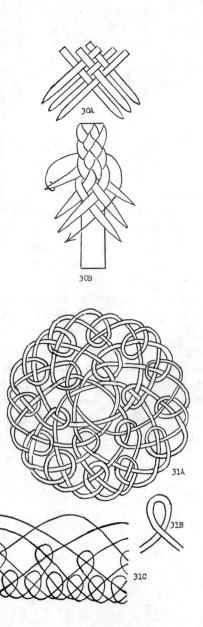

Danish book on rope-work. Being intrigued with the pattern of interlaced Half-loops (Figure 31*A*) the writer carried out some experiments. By projecting the 'mat' cylindrically another dimension was added. This appeared as in Figure No. 31*C*. As this did not give a pleasing result a similar design was superimposed with the result as shown in Figure 31*D*. Figure 31*E* shows the completed Single-cord Half-loop Decorative Turk's-Head.

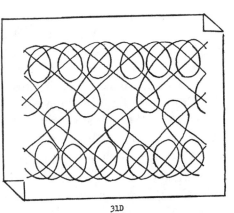

31D

Method of construction: The knot can be made with any number of Half-loops from three upwards. Figure 31*D* has been worked with six as the basic number, and the Diagram is suitable for a Bellrope with a 4″ circumference. On a piece of tracing paper trace or draw a diagram on a scale sufficient to encircle the Bellrope. Attach this diagram to the Bellrope with four equally spaced rubber bands. Take a long length of cord, and with it duplicate the design on the tracing paper, holding the Half-loops in position with the elastic bands. When the design has been completed remove the tracing paper and the rubber bands. The first lead may be followed several times, or the first cord may be flanked by cords of another colour. The ends are gummed and hidden.

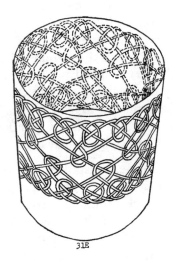

31E

No. 32. *The United Crowns Decorative Turk's-Head.* This Turk's-Head is attractive not only for its appearance but for the intriguing manner in which the Crowns are united. Any diagram with an even number of crossings is a potential Crown for a Turk's-Head. The selected Crown may have to be modified as in Figures 32*A* and 32*B*. The strands must leave one Crown in the direction of the other Crown that is to be united. In the example illustrated Crowns 32*B* and 32*C* are suitable for the purpose.

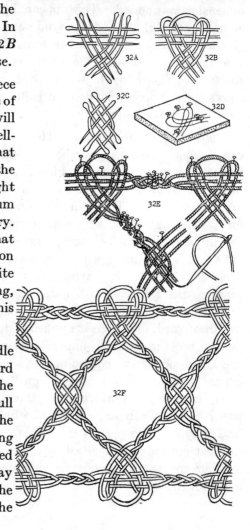

Method of construction: On a piece of tracing paper trace or draw copies of Crowns 32*B* and 32*C*. Their scale will be dependent on the girth of the Bellrope to be decorated. On a Cork mat or similar arrangement pin out the twelve Crowns that are required, eight of No. 32*B* and four of 32*C*. Gum them and leave them a while to dry. Then remove them from the Cork mat (Figure 32*D*) and pin them in position on the Bellrope (Figure 32*E*). Unite the ends with ordinary Platting, pinning the ends in position. This requires considerable care.

The next step is to thread a needle with a long length of attractive cord and work it through the design until the ends meet. To facilitate this work pull most of the cord through the eye of the needle. This gives a short working length. The long end may be pulled through separately and the kinks may be taken out as required. When the design has been completed with the

attractive cord remove the 'guide'.
Tighten up any slackness. The original
lead may be followed as many times as
required, or it may be flanked with
cord or silk of another colour. The
finished work is shown in Figures 32*F*
and 32*G*. As the gummed pattern has
to be destroyed it is as well to make it
with inferior material; and it is better
to have it in a contrasting colour.

No. **33.** *A United Designs Decorative Turk's-Head.* This is a more
ambitious project than No. 32. Three
Designs are to be united. Design 33*B*
has been modified from Design 33*A*.
Design 33*D* is a four-strand version of
Figure 32*C*; and Design 33*C* is the
famous Carrick Bend. Twenty-four
Designs are united with 4-strand Sennit
to form a Decorative Turk's-Head.
The method of construction is similar to
that described for Turk's-Head No. 32.
The writer used this Turk's-Head,
among others, on the Bellrope that won
First Prize in the 1961 Seafarers'
Education Service Annual Handicraft
Competition. Although the weave of
the cords is over-and-under the cords
from the circular Design to the Carrick
Bends, and between the Carrick Bends,
go over-over or under-under before
resuming the usual weave. This is to
prevent twisting and enables the Designs to lie flat without being stitched.

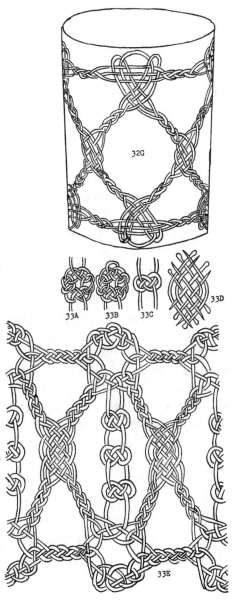

Figure 33*E* shows a considerable portion of the finished United Designs Decorative Turk's-Head; and Figure No. 97. is an illustration of the Prize Winning Bellrope where the knot is employed.

No. 34. *Single-cord Turk's-Head with an interwoven Crown.* For a three-strand Platting three strands of the Crown must lead in both directions. Figure 34*A* has been modified to Figure 34*B*. Method of construction: With a sheet of tracing paper trace or draw the Crown. Transfer the tracing to a Cork mat or other arrangement and pin the cord over the tracing. Use an inferior cord for this purpose and of a colour different to that which will be used

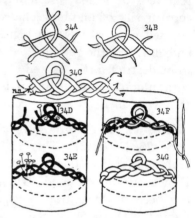

subsequently. Gum the worked Crown and leave it a while to dry. When dry transfer it to the Bellrope and pin it in position (Figure 34*D*). Plat the cords on one side of the Crown until they meet the cords on the other side of the Crown. Pin them so that they join as Platting (Figure 34*E*). Thread a needle with a length of attractive cord and follow the lead of the pattern until the two ends meet (Figure 34*F*). Remove the pattern. Tighten up any slackness. The first lead may be followed as many times as necessary, or it may be flanked with cord or silk of another colour. Figure 34*G* shows the finished Single-cord Turk's-Head with interwoven Crown.

No. 35. The Crown illustrated here
is suitable for a Single-cord Turk's-Head
with interwoven Crown. The method of
construction is described in No. 34.

No. 36. The Crowns illustrated here
have opposite leads, one being right-
handed, the other left-handed.

No. 37. On a Bellrope with a large
circumference two Crowns of different
design may conveniently be interwoven
into one Turk's-Head. Figure 37 shows
two aspects of the two Crowns when
united.

No. 38. Figure 38*A* is another
example of a Crown that is suitable for
weaving into a Turk's-Head. In Figure
38*B* this Crown has been used twice and
they are united with 4-strand Platting.

No. 39. *The Single-cord Star Knot Turk's-Head.* This is an original knot and was developed by the writer. It has never before been seen in print. The need for it must have been felt by knotsmen for a long time. It quite replaces the cumbersome Star Shroud Knot. It is particularly suitable for encircling Bellropes as there are no unsightly ends to be hidden by other Turk's-Heads. The size of the cord with which the knot is made is immaterial as one has only to increase or decrease the number of 'points' in the Star to encircle the Bellrope. Method of construction: Secure the cord to a pencil with a Cow Hitch (Figure 39*A*). Follow the sequence shown in Figures 39*B* and 39*C*.

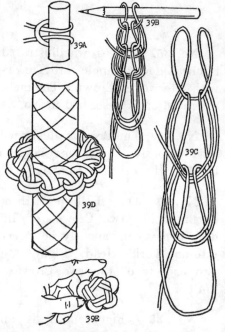

When one complete cycle has been made take up all the slack and tighten it before proceeding with the next cycle. When a sufficient number of 'points' have been made to encircle the Bellrope, make the 'locking point'. This is when the cord passes through the loops of the Cow Hitch. The result is a particularly handsome and distinguished Turk's-Head. This knot was used in the writer's entry for the 1962 Seafarers' Education Service Annual Handicraft Competition and won First Prize.

No. 40. Many designs of two-dimensional knots may be adapted to form decorative Turk's-Heads. The development is shown in the illustrations. A tracing, or scale drawing, attached to the Bellrope may be used as a guide. The work may be made to look more attractive if it is commenced with white cord and outlined with coloured silk.

No. 41. This illustration shows the effect after the two-dimensional knot has been made on a cylinder and then flattened.

No. 42. Here a similar design has been inverted above the first design and the two joined.

No. 43. The resultant effect makes an attractive Turk's-Head.

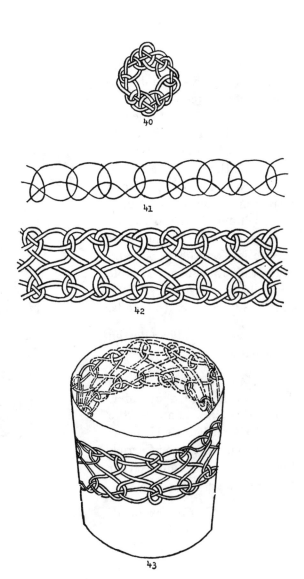

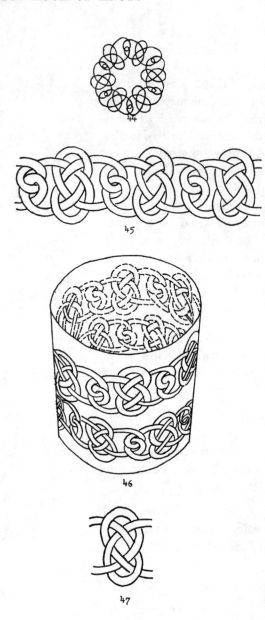

No. 44. This two-dimensional knot makes an attractive Turk's-Head when projected cylindrically. It may be easily extended or reduced. To extend shift the tracing and add designs as required. Attach a tracing, or scale drawing, to the Bellrope with a rubber band and work the knot over the design on the paper and under the rubber band. Double or treble if desired. Work taut, and 'scatter' the ends.

No. 45. The above design flattened out.

No. 46. Two rows of the design worked on a cylinder. This has been named the Carrick Bend Turk's-Head as that ancient knot, the Carrick Bend, has been employed in the design.

No. 47. *The Carrick Bend.*

No. 48. This is one of the most attractive and useful Turk's-Heads; but its construction from memory is difficult. Illustrations of it, in plan, although easy to follow are difficult to construct if one wishes to extend the number of bights at the rims. Projected cylindrically, as in the illustrations, extension is simple. Having made a tracing, shift the paper until the end of the tracing covers another complete sequence and trace that.

To construct, encircle the Bellrope with the tracing or scale drawing, securing it with a rubber band and working the cord under-and-over the guide lines and under the rubber band.

No. 49. The Turk's-Head worked on a cylinder.

No. 50. This practical Turk's-Head is made with two lengths of cord. Encircle the part of the Bellrope to be decorated with a tracing or scale drawing of the illustration and hold it in place with a rubber band; then work the cords over the guide lines and under the rubber band. Remove the paper when complete. The cords may then be doubled or trebled. Work taut and 'scatter' the ends. A dab of gum keeps them in place effectively.

No. 51. The completed Turk's-Head.

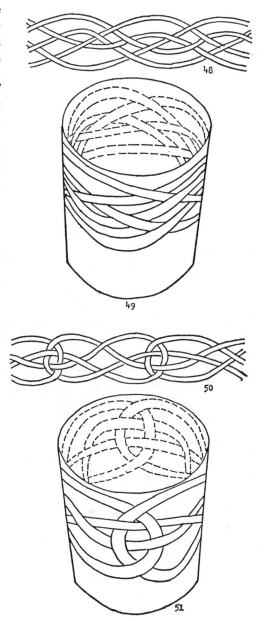

For those who may only infrequently have occasion to tie Turk's-Heads the committing to memory of the method of tying them would be a difficult task; and even following the method previously described may not prove easy. For such persons the author has projected the Common and Compound Turk's-Heads cylindrically. The method of tying knots on this projection has been explained several times previously, but for those interested only in these particular knots it is described again. Each Turk's-Head is shown with the cylindrically tied knot flattened out. To tie the knot make a tracing, or scale drawing, on a strip of paper and encircle that part of the Bellrope to be decorated with it until both ends of the drawing meet. Hold the paper in place with a rubber band. There will now be a complete representation of the Turk's-Head to act as a guide. Take a suitable length of cord, thread it through a large needle and work it along the guide lines, over and under, keeping it in place under the rubber band. When one turn has been completed remove the paper and rubber band and work the knot taut; then double or treble as required. Cut the ends of the cord so that they do not appear on the surface. A dab of gum will effectively hold them in place.

No. 52. *The Common Turk's-Head.*

No. 53. *The Compound Turk's-Head.*

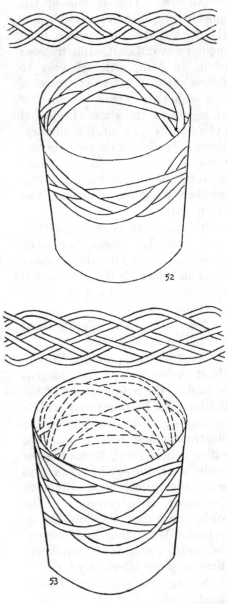

No. 55. This handsome Bellrope was decorated with Single-cord Star Knot Sennit and with a Single-cord Star Knot Turk's-Head (No. 39). This original knotting was incorporated in the entry submitted for the 1962 Annual Handicraft Competition of The Seafarers' Education Service, the First Prize being awarded jointly to Mr. J. M. Nunnerley, A.B. and the author. The rope was tapered at one end and a Spindle Eye formed. This was covered with 3-Strand Coxcombing, the ends of the Coxcombing being concealed with a Common Turk's-Head. A Manrope Knot was formed at the other end of the Bellrope and covered with a Compound Turk's-Head. After making a suitable length of Single-cord Star Knot Sennit it was twisted round the Bellrope and the ends stitched to the rope. Five strands of the same cord with which the Sennit was made were rove through the Bellrope at each end of the Sennit and Five-Point Star Knots worked. These hid the rough ends of the Sennit. Below the Sennit a Single-cord Star Knot was formed, and above the Sennit a Common Turk's-Head. The sequence for the Single-cord Star Knot Turk's-Head and Sennit is shown in the adjoining sketch.

CHAPTER VI

ON THE RAISING OF SINGLE-CORD TURK'S-HEADS TO LARGER DIMENSIONS

In the last Chapter it was stated that for practical purposes the Compound Turk's-Head was the most complicated Single-Cord Turk's-Head needed, the Built-up Turk's-Head supplying the need where a longer Turk's-Head was required. But where time is no object—and Dr. Samuel Johnson said of knotting that it was next to mere idleness—and where the most handsome work is sought then it is better to decorate with Single-cord Turk's-Heads of large dimensions. There are three classes of these Turk's-Heads: The Square, The Narrow, and The Long; and each class is raised in a different manner.

The dimensions of Turk's-Heads may be increased **both** in their length along the Bellrope and in their girth: by their length by an increased number of Turns and in their girth by an increased number of Bights. Every circuit that the cord makes round the Bellrope is called a Turn and every curve at the rim is called a Bight.

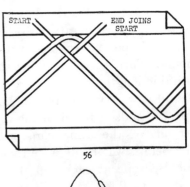

56

As far as is known the method explained here of raising the dimensions of Single-cord Turk's-Heads is the first time that such an explanation has been given. It should not be thought that there is any lessening in achievement in making the knots in this manner: for they are impossible to make from memory, and the most expert knotsman must use some method to guide him.

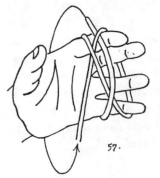

57.

28

Some of these methods treat the subject in mathematical terms; none is easy to follow. The writer has had the benefit of other authors' works and has tried to improve on their methods. Whilst he could not do this mathematically he hopes that he has graphically.

Square Turk's-Heads. In the Square Turk's-Heads described in this book the number of Turns is always one more than the number of Bights. The basic knot is the Simple Turk's-Head (No. 57) which consists of **3** Turns and 2 Bights. Two other methods of making this knot have been described in the previous chapter; that of tying it directly on the hand and that of tying it by the Cylindrical Projection. It is shown here by the Diagrammatic Method of Raising the Dimensions of Single-cord Turk's-Heads.

No. 56. Construction of a Simple Turk's-Head by the method: Measure the circumference of that part of the Bellrope to be decorated and draw a parallelogram on a piece of paper with the other two sides half this measure-

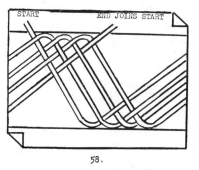

58.

ment. Within the parallelogram draw a scale reproduction of Figure No. 56 and encircle the Bellrope with it making sure that the lines on each side of the paper meet exactly. Hold the paper in place with two rubber bands, one at the top and one at the bottom of the drawing.

Take a suitable length of cord and attach it to the upper left-hand of the drawing by passing it under the rubber band; then follow the lines on the drawing with the cord, passing over and under where it is indicated.

When the end of the drawing has been reached with the cord remove the paper, arrange the Bights and various crossings of the cord equidistantly, and work the knot taut. The result will be a

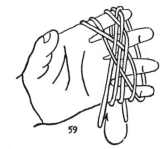

59

Simple Turk's-Head consisting of 3 Turns and 2 Bights. The knot may be doubled or trebled by following exactly the original turns once or twice more.

No. 57. The Simple Turk's-Head of 3 Turns and 2 Bights.

No. 58. Instructions for raising the dimensions of a Simple Turk's-Head of 3 Turns and 2 Bights to a Compound Turk's-Head of 5 Turns and 4 Bights. Each time two parallel lines are added to Figure No. 56, as in Figure No. 58. another complete knot is formed; and two Turns and two Bights added. It is convenient to make the paper extend slightly above and below the drawing to facilitate withdrawing it when the knot has been made.

No. 59. The Compound Turk's-Head of 5 Turns and 4 Bights.

No. 60. Instructions for raising the dimensions of a Simple Turk's-Head of 3 Turns and 2 Bights to a knot of 9 Turns and 8 Bights. The process is demonstrably simple. Six more lines have been added to the diagram in Figure No. 56, as shown in Figure No. 60.

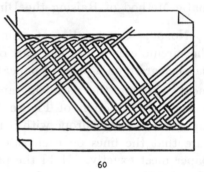

60

With the larger Turk's-Heads it will be necessary to keep the Bights in position as the work proceeds either by pinning them or by keeping them under a tight rubber band. A Turk's-Head of this description makes an admirable covering for the ends of Round Sennit, Coachwhipping or Spanish Hitching. If it is made with white cord and then outlined with coloured cord or silk it 'brings out' the work and increases its attractiveness.

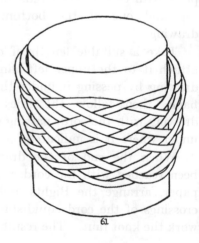

61

Narrow Turk's-Heads. A Narrow Turk's-Head is one in which the number of Bights always exceeds the number of

Turns. The number of Bights may be in excess by as many as one wishes, as in No. 63, but never less than by two.

The diagrammatic method of tying the knot which is explained here—perhaps for the first time—requires some considerable preparation, but it simplifies the work of the actual tying of the knot. The drawing of the diagram shown in Figure No. 63 took the author ten minutes.

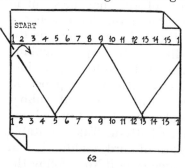

62

No. 61. A Single-cord Turk's-Head of 9 Turns and 8 Bights.

No. 62. *Construction*: Measure accurately the circumference of the part of the Bellrope to be decorated. On a piece of paper draw a parallelogram with this measurement horizontally and approximately a third of it vertically. Let the paper extend a little above and below the drawing to facilitate withdrawing when the knot is completed.

Divide the upper and lower horizontal lines and number them. From No. 1 (The Start) draw diagonal lines from side to side; and it is the number of diagonals that decides the compactness of a knot.

To obtain the spacing of the diagonals divide the number of divisions by the number of diagonals that are desired, four being the minimum. The dividend, to the nearest whole number, is the number of divisions, or spaces, along the opposite side to advance the diagonal. Example: In Figure No. 62 there are 15 divisions. $15 : 4 = 3\frac{3}{4}$ (approx.).

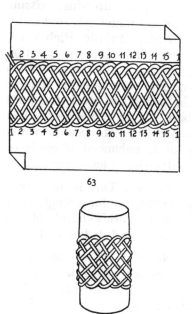

63

64

The nearest whole number is 4. Commencing at No. 1 on the upper line, draw a diagonal line to No. 5 on the lower line, and thence to 9 upper, 13 lower, and finally to 2 upper to commence the second series parallel with the first.

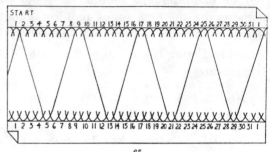

65

Having completed the criss-cross of diagonal lines, fill in the over-and-under sequence as in Figure No. 63. Encircle the Bellrope with the paper making sure that both edges join exactly. Hold the paper in place with two stout rubber bands, one at the top and one at the bottom. Take a suitable length of cord, middle it, and commencing at No. 1, follow the lines on the drawing, passing over-and-under where it is indicated. As the Bights are formed hold them in position under the rubber bands. When the knot is completed remove the paper and work the knot taut. It may then be doubled or trebled. The beauty of the knot is enhanced if cords of contrasting colours are used.

No. 63. This is the complete diagram for a Single-cord Narrow Turk's-Head of 15 divisions and 4 diagonals.

No. 64. The completed Single-cord Narrow Turk's-Head of 15 divisions and 4 diagonals.

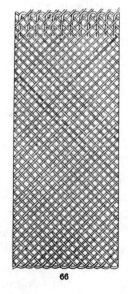

66

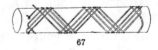

67

No. 65. This is a diagram for a Single-cord Narrow Turk's-Head of 31 divisions and 8 diagonals. The sequences are as follows: 1 upper, 5 lower, 9 upper, 13 lower, 17 upper, 21 lower, 25 upper, 29 lower, and 2 upper to commence the second series parallel with the first.

Long Turk's-Heads. In Long Turk's-Heads the number of Turns always exceed the number of Bights.

No. 66. The above statement applies to Single-cord Long Turk's-Heads. A Turk's-Head of any length can be tied with a Built-up Turk's-Head. (Figure 27, Page 13.) This may also be tied by the Diagrammatic method. *Construction*: Measure the area the Turk's-Head is to cover. Along the centre line of a drawing of this measure an equal number of spaces, each space being sufficient to take three parts of the cord it is intended to use. Make criss-cross lines through the central points at an angle of 45°. These guide-lines will indicate how many separate cords will be required. The illustration shows 12. Round each bight at the top as indicated. The base can be terminated wherever required. When the under-over pattern is completed wrap the diagram round the Bellrope and secure it at top and bottom with rubber bands. Attach with adhesive tape one cord for each upper bight and follow the pattern passing over and under where it is indicated. It assists if the cord is threaded through a suitably sized needle. Advance each cord one tuck at a time. When the work is completed the knot will have covered the paper.

No. 67. This is a diagram showing part of the construction of a Single-cord Long Turk's-Head consisting of 12 bights and 31 turns.

No. 68. A really ambitious project is the tying of this Single-cord Long Turk's-Head of 12 bights and 31 turns. An expert knotsman would need some form of guide to tie such an intricate knot. As good a guide as any is the diagrammatic method shown here. Unlike the Built-up pattern, which can be terminated on any line, with the Single-cord knot an exact copy of the pattern must be drawn in the area required for the knot. Measure the area and draw it on a sheet of thin paper. Along the top and bottom edges make 12 bights. One of the bights at both ends will be divided, a half on either side. Down the central line make 30 equally spaced divisions. With a ruler connect these to the bights. Complete the drawing showing the under-over pattern. Wrap the paper round the Bellrope making sure that both sides meet correctly. Secure at top and bottom with rubber bands. Wind a spiral of adhesive tape round the paper, sticky side uppermost. Using a cord, three parts of which will

Fig. 68

occupy one 'square' or 'diamond', start
anywhere and follow the pattern. The
sticky surface will keep the cord in place.

No. 69. An attractive Bellrope on
which three of the Turk's-Heads dis-
cussed in this Chapter have been
employed.

The rope used was 3-strand sisal. It
was tapered at both ends. At the upper
end a Spindle Eye was formed and at the
other end several of the yarns were cut
out and the strands then canvas covered.
The rope was then wormed and parcelled
and served. The Spindle Eye was
covered with 3-strand Coxcombing and
a thimble was inserted in the Eye. A
length of Palm and Needle Hitching was
worked from the Spindle Eye and from
the canvas covered strands. The strands
were then formed into a Manrope Knot.
The 'canvas' was now ready to be
'painted'.

No. 70. A Single-cord Square Turk's-
Head.

No. 71. A Single-cord Narrow Turk's-
Head.

No. 72. A Built-up Turk's-Head
similar to Figure 66.

CHAPTER VII

KNOB KNOTS

No. 73. The most decorative and complicated, and certainly the most distinctive Knob Knot is the Star Knot; and to be able to make it is a considerable achievement. The Star Knob Knot is generally made with a minimum of five strands and a maximum of eight. Grasp the stem in the left hand. Commence by forming a Half Hitch with each strand and passing the end of the strand through the loop of the next Half Hitch to the right. Work the Half Hitches up snugly to the centre (Figure 73A).

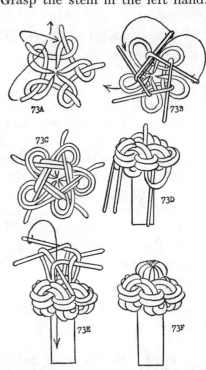

Form a Left-hand Crown with all the strands. Figure 73B shows the completed Left-hand Crown. Tuck each strand back above the loop of the Half Hitch and under its own part. With each strand in turn follow the lead inside the adjoining strand to the right, over one Half Hitch, and down through the loop of the next Half Hitch. Figure 73C shows the knot at this stage, and Figure 73D shows another view of it. Continue to follow the lead underneath the knot and tuck each strand in turn up through the centre. (Figure 73D).

When all the strands have been tucked up through the centre of the knot, form a Right-hand Crown with all of them. (Figure 73E). Take each strand in turn and tuck it down through the centre of the knot. (Figure 73E). Draw all the strands up snugly so as to give an even rounded effect to the knot. Cut the ends of the strands off close to the work and put a dab of gum on them to prevent them from fraying. Figure 73F shows the finished Star Knob Knot.

The next three Knob Knots are a combination of Walling and Crowning (See Chapter 2). The strands are first Walled, generally to the right, and a Crown, also to the right, is superimposed.

No. 74. *A Five-strand Wall-and-Crown Knob Knot.* Commence by seizing the strands with a Constrictor Knot (No. 10). Then Wall all the strands to the right (Figure 74B). Punch a number of holes in a piece of paper corresponding to the pattern that it is intended to use and pass the ends of the Walled strands up through these holes. (Figure 74B). This enables the Crown to be made without interference from the Walling below it. Having made the Crown (Figure 74C) remove the paper and take up the slack on the Wall and the Crown. With the strands that emerge from the Crown follow the first lead of the Wall. (Figure 74D). Continue to follow the lead as many times as required. Figure 74E shows the completed Five-strand Wall-and-Crown Knob Knot.

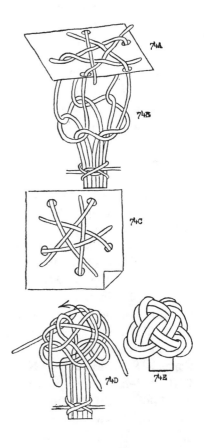

No. 75. This is another account of the Five-strand Wall-and-Crown Knob Knot, No. 74 being in elevation, this account being in plan. Figure 75A shows the five strands Walled to the right. Figure 75B shows the strands

emerging through the holes in the paper and formed into a fanciful Crown. In Figure 75C the paper has been removed and the Crown can be seen super-imposed over the Wall. The direction that the Crowned strands take in follow-ing the lead of the Wall is indicated by the arrows. Figure 75D is an end-on view of the finished Five-strand Wall-and-Crown Knob Knot.

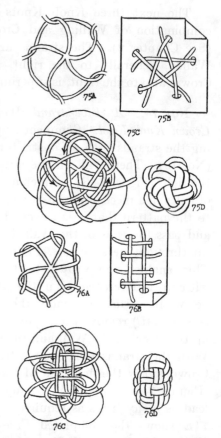

No. 76.   *A Six-strand Wall-and-Crown Knob Knot.* The Crown used for this knot is the famous Spritsail Sheet Knot.   Seize six strands with a Con-strictor Knot (No. 10).   Wall all the strands to the right. (Figure 76A). Punch holes in a piece of paper corres-ponding to the pattern of the Spritsail Sheet Knot and pass the ends of the Walled strands up through these holes. Form a Spritsail Sheet Knot. (Figure 76B).   Remove the paper and take up the slack on the Walling and Crowning and with the strands that emerge from the Crown follow the first lead of the Wall.   Figure 76A shows the six strand Walled to the right.   Figure 76B shows the strands emerging through the holes in the paper and formed into a Spritsail Sheet Knot Crowned.   In Figure 76C the paper has been removed and the Crown can be seen super-imposed over the Wall.   The direction that the Crowned strands take in following the lead of the Wall is indicated by the arrows.   Figure 76D shows an end-on view of the finished Six-strand Wall-and-Crown Knob Knot.

No. 77. *An Eight-strand Wall-and-Crown Knob Knot.* This is one of the most useful and effective Knob Knots for finishing Continuous-cord Bellropes. In spite of the complicated appearance of the illustrations it is easily and quickly made. Seize eight strands with a Constrictor Knot (No. 10). Wall all the strands to the right. (Figure 77*A*). Punch holes with the tip of a pencil in a piece of paper corresponding to the pattern illustrated in Figure 77*B* and pass the ends of the Walled strands up through these holes. Form the Crown. (Figure 77*B*). Remove the paper and take up the slack on the Walling and Crowning, and with the strands that emerge from the Crown follow the first lead of the Wall. Figure 77*A* shows the eight strands Walled to the right. Figure 77*B* shows the eight strands emerging through the holes in the paper and formed into a fanciful Crown. In Figure 77*C* the paper has been removed

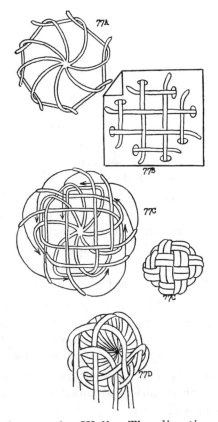

and the Crown can be seen superimposed over the Wall. The direction Crowned strands take in the following that the lead of the Wall is indicated by arrows. Figure 77*D* shows an end-on view of the finished Eight-strand Wall-and-Crown Knob Knot. To make the Knob Knot more bulbous make a ball of tightly bound string and insert it between the Walling and Crowning before the strands are drawn up taut. This is shown in the illustration in Figure 77*D*. The cut off ends of the strands are gummed to prevent them from fraying or working loose, and they are hidden from view.

CHAPTER VIII

THE COVERED-ROPE BELLROPE
Construction

At the risk of being considered facetious it is the writer's opinion that the most important thing about the making of Bellropes, or for that matter of anything else, is to start! That is the reason I have shown in the first illustration a hand grasping a length of rope. It is this that we have to mould and work on to achieve the result depicted at the end of this explanation.

No. 78. Having taken a suitable length of rope we can now proceed with the work. A 24″ length of 2¾″ sisal rope would do admirably. In the illustration the lay of the rope is right-handed, but left-handed rope would do as well.

No. 79. Taper the rope at one end. Unlay the rope for 9″ and seize with a Constrictor Knot (No. 10). With a sharp knife or scissors reduce the yarns in each strand by one third. There are 20 yarns in each strand. Lay up the rope again for 3″ and seize it again. Then further reduce the strands until sixteen remain. The end is now ready to form the Spindle Eye.

40

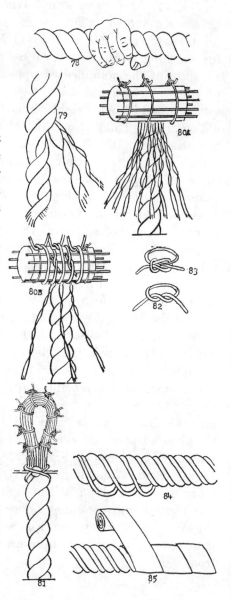

No. 80. *The Spindle Eye.* Take a cylinder with a circumference a little larger than the Thimble (No. 88) that it is intended to insert and along it attach several short lengths of twine (Figure 80*A*). These are for the subsequent binding of the yarns that form the Spindle Eye. (See Figure 81). A suitable cylinder may be made with a rolled magazine secured with adhesive tape. Place the cylinder, or spindle, above the sixteen parted ropeyarns and bring the ropeyarns round the cylinder, joining them with a Half Knot (Figure 82). See that the Half Knots are placed evenly round the cylinder. With the prepared short lengths of twine (Figure 80*A*) bind the ropeyarns surrounding the cylinder together securing them with Reef Knots (Figure 83). Remove the cylinder.

No. 82. *A Half Knot.* Used to join the ropeyarns round the cylinder, or spindle.

No. 83. *A Reef Knot.* Used to secure the twine when binding the ropeyarns that form the Spindle Eye.

No. 84. *Worming.* To give the rope a rounded finish it is necessary to fill in the seams of the rope. This is known as Worming. The ropeyarns that have been removed in the Tapering may be used for this purpose. Five in each seam will make an effective Worming. Worm the seams for 7″ from the Spindle Eye and secure both ends with adhesive tape.

No. 85. *Parcelling.* This is a form of bandaging and further adds to the smoothness and roundness of the Bellrope. Parcelling is always done in the same direction as the Worming. Adhesive tape is a good material for Parcelling.

No. 86. *Serving.* To give firmness and extra girth to the Bellrope the Worming and Parcelling is Served, or bound with cord. The direction of the Serving is always opposite to that of the Worming and Parcelling, and against the lay of the rope.

No. 87. *Coxcombing the Spindle Eye.* Until now inferior material and odds and ends have been used: but the exposed work must be done with the most handsome material available. Up-end the Bellrope and attach three lengths of cord to one side of the Spindle Eye and cast on to the Eye alternate right and left Half Hitches as in the illustration. (Figure 87*A*). Secure the ends with a Constrictor Knot. Figure 87*B*). Trim the ends and insert the Thimble. (Figure 87*C*).

No. 88. *The Thimble*. This is inserted in the Spindle Eye. The Bellrope is attached to the clanger of the bell with a shackle. The Thimble prevents the shackle from chafing the Coxcombing.

The Knob Knot at the other end of the Bellrope is the next thing to be dealt with. Unlay the strands as far as the Serving and cut out one-third of the ropeyarns in each strand.

No. 89. *Canvas covering the strands*. Prepare three 15″ lengths of duck canvas or linen each 2¼″ wide. Make a hem on each side ½″ wide. Press with a hot iron. With needle and cotton sew the canvas round the strands that will form the Knob Knot.

No. 90. *The Knob Knot*. The illustration is of a Manrope Knot. With the three canvas covered strands make a **Right-hand Wall** (Figure No. 7). **Above** it make a Right-hand Crown (Figure No. 8). Follow round the Wall and Crown two or three times. It will

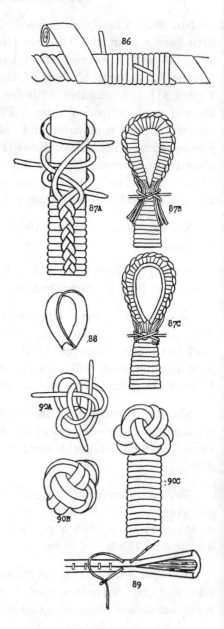

be necessary to keep twisting the strands so that the seams of the canvas are always hidden from view. Cut the ends of the strands close to the knot and scatter them. This is done by drawing the strand taut before cutting it and then hiding the end under the strands that pass over it. Figure 90*A* shows the strands Walled and Crowned to the right. Figure 90*B* is an end-on view of the finished Manrope Knot; and Figure 90*C* is a side view of it.

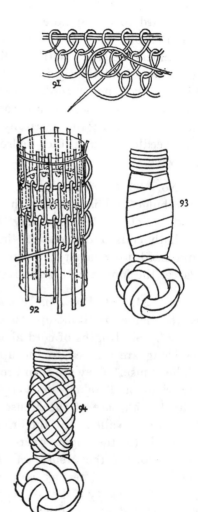

No. 91. *Palm and Needle Hitching.* Return to the Spindle Eye end of the Bellrope. Work 1½″ of Palm and Needle Hitching. Start with two loops of the cord round the Bellrope and secure it by reeving the needle through the rope. Cast a series of Hitches on to the loops and continue hitching to the Hitches themselves. When sufficient work is done, secure by reeving the needle and cord through the Bellrope once or twice. Coloured macramé cord is very effective for this work.

No. 92. *Spanish Hitching.* Below the Palm and Needle Hitching secure a number of cords about 18″ long around the circumference of the Bellrope. The cords should be placed closely together. Thread a needle with a length of somewhat finer cord. Knot the end and reeve the needle and cord through the Bellrope where the cords have been secured. The knot is drawn into the Bellrope where it will be secure. Attach a lanyard to the Spindle Eye and hang the Bellrope so that the work is at a convenient height. With the finer cord as a warp held tightly in the left hand hitch each hanging cord in turn round it. The work builds up easily and quickly. Secure the warp by reeving the needle through the Bellrope once or twice.

No. 93 *Raising a Mouse.* A Mouse is a bulge and is raised with twine or cord. Let it be gradually tapering at both ends and about 2″ in length, and hard up against the Knob Knot. Parcel the Mouse with adhesive tape.

No. 94. *A Pineapple Knot.* This is the same as Built-up Turk's-Head No. 27. Six lengths of cord about three feet long are secured to the upper end of the Mouse. They are then Crowned to the right and taken in a right-hand helix to the base of the Mouse. There they are Walled to the right and spiralled to the right over-and-under to the top of the Mouse. Follow the lead as many times as required. It adds to the beauty if the cord is outlined with coloured silk or thread.

No. 95. Add Common Turk's-Head No. 22.

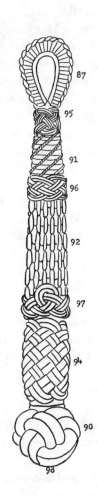

No. 96. Add Compound Turk's-Head No. 21.

No. 97. Add Single-cord Turk's-Head with an interwoven Crown No. 34.

No. 98. The finished Bellrope. This would be a credit to any bell.

No. 106. *A Covered-rope Bellrope.* This introduces two more rope coverings: Grafting and Pointing. Prepare the rope as explained in this Chapter. Coxcomb the Spindle Eye (Figure 87) and insert the Thimble (Figure 88). Add 1½″ of Grafting.

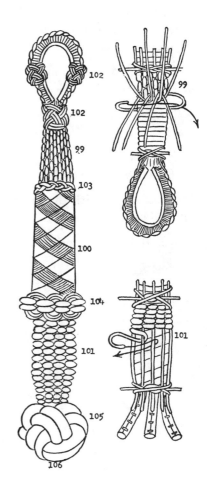

No. 99. *Grafting.* Secure an even number of cords to the Bellrope with a Constrictor Knot (No. 10). In the same position as the Constrictor Knot reeve a 2 foot length of cord. This is the warp. Divide the cords and extend each alternate cord holding the other to the stem. Wind the warp round the intersection of the divided cords and pass the end of the warp through its own bight. This is known as a Half Hitch. Then turn down the cords that were extended and extend those that were held against the stem; and again wind and Half Hitch the warp. Complete the work by reeving the warp through the Bellrope for greater security.

No. 100. Work 2½″ of 4-Strand Coachwhipping with a spiral pattern (No. 28). Below this work 2″ of Pointing.

No. 101. *Pointing.* Below the Coach-whipping seize a number of cords to the Bellrope with a Constrictor Knot (No. 10). Stretch these to the base of the Bellrope and seize them again. Near the top Constrictor Knot reeve a 2 foot length of cord. This is the warp. Using a needle make an overhand round-turn with the warp round each stretched cord until the space is completed. Reeve the warp through the Bellrope for greater security.

No. 102. Add a Common Turk's-Head (No. 22) on each side of the Spindle Eye and one at the Neck.

No. 103. Add simple Turk's-Head No. 20 between the Grafting and the Coachwhipping.

No. 104. Work a Single-cord Star Knot Turk's-Head (No. 39) between the Coachwhipping and the Pointing.

No. 105A. With the prepared strands complete the Bellrope with Knob Knot No. 90.

No. 106B. The finished Bellrope.

CHAPTER IX

THE CONTINUOUS-CORD BELLROPE

Construction

Bellropes that are used in the open need to be painted. If they are not the weather soon deteriorates them. The Continuous-cord Bellrope lends itself much better for painting than the Covered-rope type, the attractiveness being in the involved knotting and in the painting.

No. 105. Take four lengths of boat-lacing, a coarse rope about the thickness of a pencil, each being about eight feet long. Seize the four at the middle with a Constrictor Knot (No. 10) and make a sufficient length of 4-Strand Square Sennit on one side of the Knot to surround the Thimble that will be inserted in the Eye.

No. 106. *4-Strand Square Sennit.* Take three strands in the left hand and one strand in the right. Take the outer left hand strand across to the right and lay it on the inside of the right hand strand. Take the outer of the right hand pair across in front and lay it on the inside of the left hand pair. Take the outer of the three strands in the left

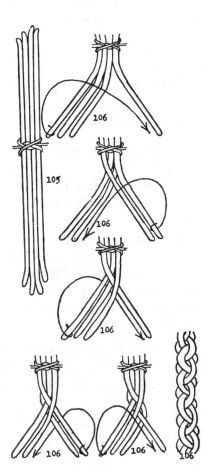

47

hand across behind and lay it on the inside of the right hand strand. Finally take the outer of the right hand pair across behind and lay it on the inside of the left hand pair. It is very simple and builds up quickly.

No. 107. Form the Eye with the length of 4-Strand Square Sennit; and with the eight strands make about $1\frac{1}{2}''$ of 8-Strand Round Sennit. Insert the Thimble into the Eye. (Figure 107*B*).

No. 108. *Round Sennit.* Extend the eight strands. Pass each alternate strand across the next strand to the right and grasp it with the left hand. Pass the still extended four strands in turn across the next strand to the left and extend the strands that were in the grasp of the hand. This is not as difficult as it may sound, and it builds up rapidly. Seize the eight strands with Constrictor Knot (No. 10).

No. 109. Make an 8-Strand Matthew Walker Knot (No. 14) over the short length of 8-Strand Round Sennit.

No. 110. Make an 8-Strand Star Knot (No. 15) below the 8-Strand Matthew Walker Knot.

No. 111. Make two or so inches of 8-Strand Cross Pointing below the Star Knot. Cross Pointing is similar to

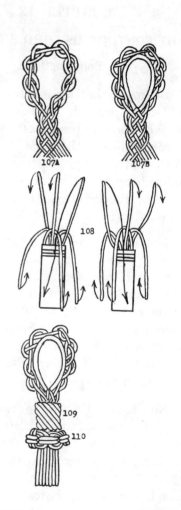

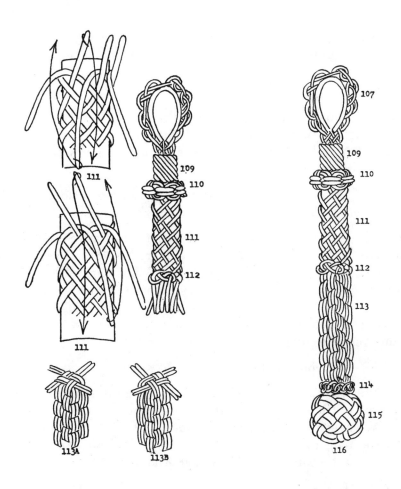

Round Sennit and Coachwhipping. The difference being that Round Sennit is made without a core, and Coachwhipping is made with a flat strand. Having made several rows of Cross Pointing insert a short length of 1" rope. This is the core over which the Cross Pointing will be built. It is worked in exactly the same way as Round Sennit (No. 108).

No. 112. Below the Cross Pointing work an 8-Strand Diamond Sennit Knot (No. 18).

No. 113. Make about 3" of 4-Strand Crown and Reverse Crown Sennit. Divide the eight strands into four pairs using each pair as a strand. Crown . the four pairs to the right and left alternately as in Figures 113A and 113B Keep the work snug.

No. 114. Below the Crown and Reverse Crown Sennit form an 8-Strand Diamond Sennit Knot (No. 17).

No. 115. Below the Diamond Sennit Knot make a 8-Strand Wall-and-Crown Knob Knot over a ball of string. (Figure No. 76). Give the Bellrope two coats of Flat White Paint and a coat of White Marine Gloss or suitable hard drying glossy paint; and when dry decorate it with whatever colours and combination of colours fancy prompts. The result will be very attractive and will last for years—even at sea when ringing the passing hours and reporting lights.

No. 116. The finished Bellrope.

No. 117. *A Continuous-cord Bellrope.* This introduces two more examples of continuous-cord knotting: 8-Strand Square Sennit and 3-Strand Crown and Reverse Crown Sennit. The Eye is 4-Strand Square Sennit (No. 106); the Neck is 8-Strand Round Sennit (No. 108); this is followed by an 8-Strand Matthew Walker Knot (No. 14).

No. 118. Below the Matthew Walker Knot make an 8-Strand Diamond Sennit Knot (No. 18). Then make a length of 8-Strand Square Sennit.

No. 119. 8-*Strand Square Sennit.* Take five strands in the left hand and three in the right. Take the outer left-hand strand and pass it across in front and lay it on the inside of the three right-hand strands. Take the outer of the four right-hand strands and pass it across in front and lay it inside the four strands in the left hand; take the outer of the five strands in the left hand and pass it across behind and lay it inside the three strands in the right hand; finally take the outer of the four strands in the right hand and pass it across behind and lay it inside the four strands in the left hand.

No. 120. Below the Square Sennit form an 8-Strand Diamond Sennit Knot (No. 16).

No. 121. With two strands form Standing Turk's-Head No. 24.

No. 122. With the remaining six strands work a length of 3-Strand Crown and Reverse Crown Sennit. Divide the six strands into three pairs and use each pair as a strand. Crown the three pairs to the right and left alternately as shown in Figures 122*A* and 122*B*.

No. 123. Below the Crown and Reverse Crown Sennit work a 6-Strand Diamond Sennit Knot. (No. 17).

No. 124. Below the Diamond Sennit Knot make a 6-Strand Star Knob Knot (No. 73).

Paint the Bellrope with two coats of Flat White Paint and one coat of Glossy White; then finish it in a flight of fancy colours.

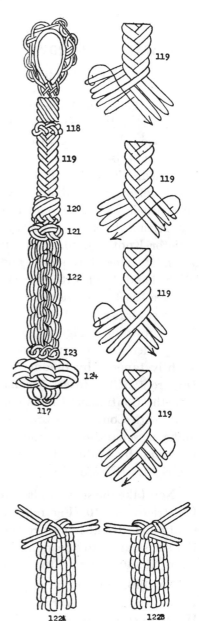

CHAPTER X

THE WALL-AND-CROWN BELLROPE

Construction

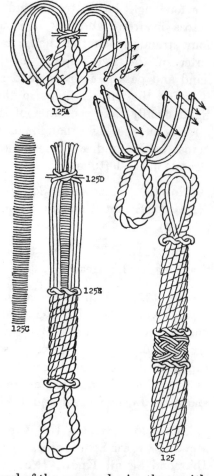

No. 125. *The Wall-and-Crown Bell-rope.* This Bellrope is ideal for small bells and is best made with a soft cotton rope as this lies more snugly when Crowned. Take an 8 foot length of good cotton rope about the thickness of a pencil. Middle it and form an Eye by seizing it at the neck with Constrictor Knot No. 10. Open up the six strands. Upend the Eye and make a Right-hand Wall with the six strands. (Figure 125*A*). Remove the seizing and make several rows of Continuous Right-hand Crowning. (Figure 125*B*). Prepare a 4½″ length of rope that has been slightly tapered by binding with twine. (Figure 125*C*). Insert the narrow end into the Continuous Crowning and continue with Continuous Crowning for 2″. Make a separation to the Continuous Crowning by Walling the six strands to the right. (Figure 125*E*).

Now take the six strands to the bulbous end of the core and seize them with Constrictor No. 10. (Figure 125*D*). Turn the Bellrope Eye upwards and work Continuous Right-hand Crowning with the six strands for about 2″. Wall the six strands to the right and secure them to the core with Constrictor Knot No. 10. Cut off the surplus ends.

No. 126. Cover the gap between the Walling with a Compound Turk's Head (No. 21). A variation can be made by the use of different Turk's-Heads to cover the gap. Insert a Thimble into the Eye.

Nautical Time	Bells	Watch		Time	Bells	Watch
2400 (Midnight)	8					
0030	1			1230	1	
0100	2			1300	2	
0130	3			1330	3	
0200	4			1400	4	
0230	5	Middle		1430	5	Afternoon
0300	6			1500	6	
0330	7			1530	7	
0345	1			1545	1	
0400	8			1600	8	
0430	1			1630	1	
0500	2			1700	2	First Dog
0530	3			1730	3	
0600	4			1800	4	
0630	5	Morning		1830	1	
0700	6			1900	2	Second, or Last, Dog
0720	7			1930	3	
0745	1			1945	1	
0800	8			2000	8	
0830	1			2030	1	
0900	2			2100	2	
0930	3			2130	3	
1000	4			2200	4	
1030	5	Forenoon		2230	5	First
1100	6			2300	6	
1120	7			2330	7	
1145	1			2345	1	
1200	8			2400	8	

TIME-KEEPING BY SHIP'S BELL

There are two exceptions to the rule that the bell is struck every thirty minutes: One bell is struck at a quarter of an hour before the end of the watch, when the relief is called; and seven bells are struck at 0720 in the Morning Watch and at 1120 in the Forenoon Watch to allow the relief sufficient time for a meal before coming on duty.

When sailors worked Watch-and-Watch (4 hours on duty and 4 hours off) the system of Dog Watches caused a daily alteration of the watch rota.

Each pair of bells is struck in rapid succession.

CHAPTER XI

THE PRIZE WINNING BELLROPE

No. 127. A Bellrope, similar to the one illustrated, won First Prize in the 1961 Seafarers' Education Service Annual Handicraft Competition. The original, which occupied the writer for six weeks on a voyage from the U.K. to the Persian Gulf and back, has a length of thirty inches. The foundation was of 4″ sisal rope and was prepared in the manner described in Chapter VIII. The Fancy-work that covered the Bellrope is listed below.

No. 128. The Spindle Eye is covered with 3-strand Coxcombing (No. 87).

No. 129. From the Spindle Eye there is a length of Palm and Needle Hitching (No. 91).

No. 130. Then follows several inches of Grafting (No. 99).

No. 131. Below the Grafting is a long length of Spanish Hitching (No. 92).

No. 132. Below the Spanish Hitching and as far as the Knob Knot is Pointing (No. 101). This completes, as it were, the 'canvas' which is now ready to be 'painted'.

128
133

133

129

134

135

130

136

137

131

133

139

140

141

142

132

143

144

127

54

No. 133. On either side of the Spindle Eye, and at the Neck, Common Turk's-Heads have been worked in white cord (No. 22). The lead has been doubled and then outlined with blue silk.

No. 134. Over the Palm and Needle Hitching is a Decorative Design as described in Chapter V, No. 33.

No. 135. Below the Decorative Design is a Single-cord Star Knot Turk's-Head (No. 39).

No. 136. On the Grafting and below the Star Knot are two 5-Strand Wall-and-Crown Knob Knots (Nos. 74 and 75) and two 5-strand Star Knob Knots (No. 73). These have been made from cords that have been reeved through the rope.

No. 137. Dividing the Grafting from the Spanish Hitching is a Square Turk's-Head of 31 Divisions and 8 Diagonals made with white cord and outlined with blue silk (No. 65).

No. 138. Below the Square Turk's-Head and on the Spanish Hitching 5-strand and 6-strand Wall-and-Crown Knob Knots encircle the Bellrope. These have been made from cords that have been reeved through the rope and as described in Chapter VII, Nos. 73, 74 and 75.

No. 139. Below the Wall-and-Crown Knob Knots and encircling the Bellrope like a chaplet is a Single-cord Turk's-Head with an Interwoven Crown (No. 34).

No. 140. Below the Interwoven Crown Turk's-Head is Single-cord Turk's-Head with Interwoven Crown, (No. 38). In this instance two Crowns have been interwoven into the one Turk's-Head. White cord outlined with blue silk.

No. 141. Below this Chinese Priest Cord designs worked in white cord have been attached to the Spanish Hitching (Chapter XIII, No. 51 and Chapter XVI, No. 3). Another decoration suitable for this space would be the Single-cord Turk's-Head described in Chapter V, No. 33.

No. 142. Dividing the Spanish Hitching from the Pointing is a Narrow Turk's-Head (No. 23).

No. 143.   Over the Pointing is a Decorative Turk's-Head formed by uniting four Chinese Priest Cord designs (Chapter XVI, No. 3).

No. 144.   The Pointing is terminated with a Diamond Sennit Knot (No. 16); the ends being encircled by a Compound Turk's-Head (No. 21) to form the Tasse!.

AN INVESTIGATION INTO THE OCCURRENCE IN GENERAL KNOTTING OF CERTAIN BASIC KNOTS

CHAPTER XII

THE OVERHAND KNOT

An interesting field of study is the ocurrence in knotting of certain basic knots. There are not many; but from these several thousands of knots have been developed. The principal ones are The Overhand and Half Knot, The Single Turn and Half Hitch, The Figure-Eight Knot and the Carrick Bend. The simplification could be taken further as there is not one of these basic knots that does not contain The Single Turn or The Half Hitch.

In the chapters that follow an attempt has been made to show what diversity of form may be obtained from very simple beginnings. No originality is claimed for the knots themselves which are well known to knotsmen. The purpose of the work is to classify knots and to show to which group they belong, and which it is hoped will give a better understanding of their structure.

No. 1. *The Overhand Knot and the Half Knot.* A length of cord of itself is a lifeless thing; but it has potentialities. As it lies supinely on the deck it consists of an End, a Bight, and a Standing Part.

No. 2. Take hold of the Bight and draw the cord along the deck and an Open Loop is formed.

No. 3. Throw the End over the Standing Part and you have a Single Turn; and where there are two parts

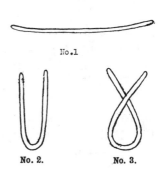

No.1

No. 2.   No. 3.

57

crossing one must be over and the other under.

No. 4. If the End of the Single Turn is passed through the Loop it produces the simplest knot of all, The Overhand Knot. The knot illustrated is a *Left-Handed Overhand Knot.*

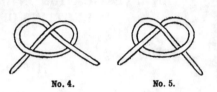

No. 4.   No. 5.

No. 5. *A Right-Handed Overhand Knot.*

No. 6. *A Slip Knot* is formed from an Overhand Knot. It acts as a Stopper Knot to prevent the rope being drawn back through an aperture, such as a Deadeye. A Noose is formed in the same manner but has another purpose: the Noose itself being passed over an object and drawn taut.

No. 6.

No. 7. *A Left-Handed Half Knot.*

No. 8. *A Right-Handed Half Knot.*

No. 9. Two Half Knots, one Left-Handed and one Right-Handed, form a *Reef* or *Square Knot.* A Reef Knot is a Binding Knot.

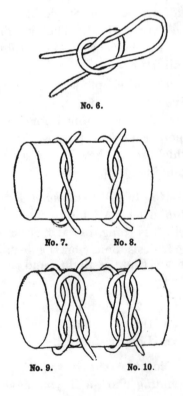

No. 7.   No. 8.

No. 10. *A Granny Knot* consists of two Left-Handed, or two Right-Handed Half Knots. It has no value as a Binding Knot but is used in decorative Square Knotting.

No. 9.   No. 10.

No. 11. If an object is inserted through the right or left-hand aperture of an Overhand Knot a Half Hitch will formed.

No. 12. *A Bowline* commences with an Overhand Knot. Form a Right-Handed Overhand Knot. Turn the Loop to the left over the Standing Part. Pass the End round the Standing Part and back through the Loop. The Bowline has many uses on board ship. A parted hawser may be made good by temporarily bending the ends together with Bowlines; Pilots' grips are hoisted and lowered by means of it; and for the making of speedy and efficient Loops in gantlines it is unsurpassed.

No. 14. *The True Lover's Knot* is formed with two Left-Handed Overhand Knots. Make the left hand one first and pass the End through its Loop before making the right-hand one. Then pass each Loop through the lower compartment of the opposite knot. This knot is used in Fancy Knotting.

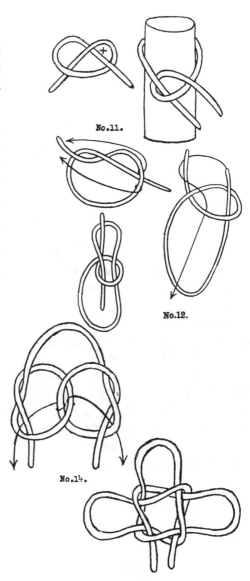

No. 11.

No. 12.

No. 14.

No. 15. *Twist Braid* or *Bugle Cord* is commenced with an Overhand Knot. With the two parts of the Loop and the End form ordinary platting or Common Sennit, drawing the End through as necessary.

No. 16. *The Ocean Plat Mat.* There are various starts to this Basket Weave Knot. This one is commenced with a Right-Handed Overhand Knot. Draw down the two Loops and make a right-hand twist with each one. Arrange them both at an angle of 45 degrees with the right Loop over the left Loop. Weave the Ends of the Overhand Knot so that the strands 'lock' over-and-under. The operation may be extended as many times as required.

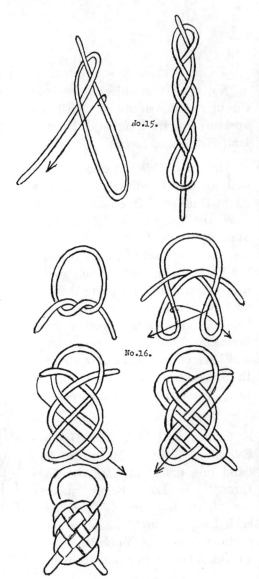

No. 17. An Overhand Knot is also a Two-Strand Crown, and as such is used to start several Two-Strand Lanyard Knots. Seize two strands and form a Right-Handed Crown by making a Right-Handed Overhand Knot. Wall the strands and pass the Ends through the compartments in the Crown, the right strand behind and the left strand in front. Walling is Crowning upside down. Draw the knot up snugly round the seizing. The knot formed is a *Two-Strand Footrope Knot.*

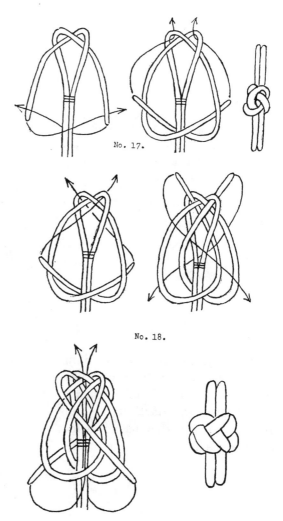

No. 17.

No. 18.

No. 18. After Crowning and Walling the two strands as in the previous example the left strand is passed through the right compartment of the Crown in front, and the right strand through the left compartment of the Crown behind. Then each strand is passed under the Bights just formed. Finally the strands cross one Standing Part and are passed up through the stem and out through the Crown. The knot formed is a *Two-Strand Footrope Knot* resembling Sennit. It appears difficult but is really quite simple. In forming the Sennit draw up each strand a little at a time.

No. 19. *The Rope Yarn Knot.*
Make two parts with both ends and
marry them. With the two lower
parts tie a Half Knot above the two
lazy parts. The knot is sufficiently
secure to unite yarns used when
serving a rope.

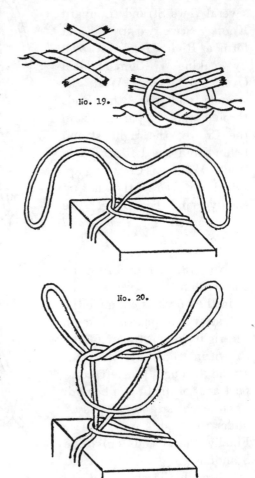

No. 20. Shortening a Sling.
After the bale or case has been
slung with a Bale Hitch form two
Loops with the slack of the sling
and form an Overhand Knot before
passing the Loops over the hook.

No. 21. *The Bowline on the Bight.* Like the Bowline this is also developed from an Overhand Knot. Make a Right-Handed Overhand Knot. Turn the Loop to the left over the Standing Part. Open the Loop and pass it completely over and round the knot until it encircles the Standing Part. Draw up snugly. This may be used as a temporary Bosun's Chair.

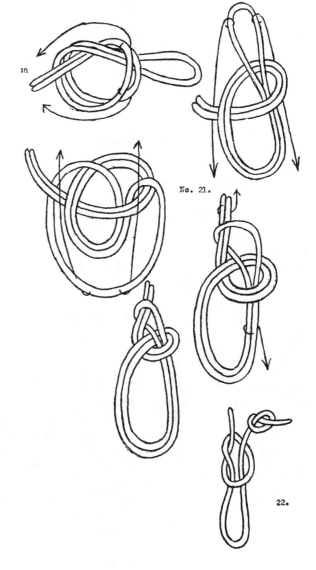

No. 21.

No. 22. A simple method of tying a *Loop* for light work. Form a Slip Knot and tie an Overhand Knot at the End of the rope. Draw up snugly.

22.

No. 23. A 'hidden' Overhand Knot is revealed in the making of an *Oval Mat*. With a cord make the pattern shown in the first illustration until the cord again lies parallel with the 'Start'. Now take the 'Start' end and follow the directions in the first illustration. The result will be as in the second illustration. At this stage if the two ends of the cord are pulled only a Right-Handed Overhand Knot will result!

The third illustration shows the completed Mat. This is the popular shipboard Mat *par excellence*. The author recently made two using 1¼-inch Point-line. One measuring 18 inches long, and 5 ply, took 65 feet of rope. The other, 22 inches long and 4 ply, took 85 feet.

No. 24. *A Platted Mat* started with an Overhand Knot. Extend the Bight of a Left-Handed Overhand Knot and give it a left-hand half twist. Lay the Standing Part over this and weave the End through. The mat may be enlarged by extending the Bight and Basket Weaving the Ends.

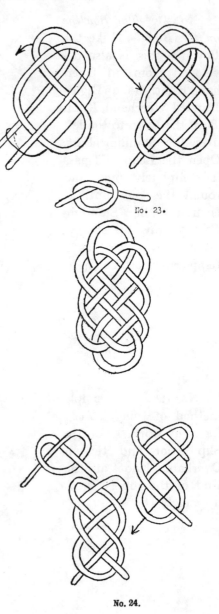

No. 23.

No. 24.

No. 25. *The Overhand Knot* itself is the simplest form of Mat. Parallel the Standing Part with the End; cut the ends short and stitch out of sight.

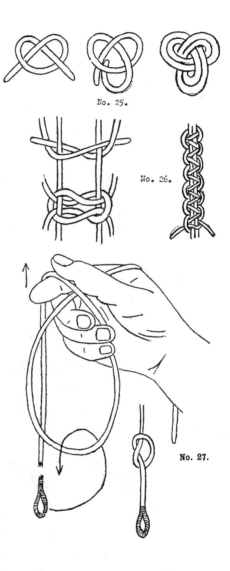

No. 25.

No. 26.

No. 26. In Square Knotting, which the sailor developed during the last century, the *Half Knot* or *Macramé Knot* is one of the two elementary knots used; the other being the Half Hitch, or Tatting Knot. Two Half Knots, one above the other, form a Solomon Knot, and a number of Solomon Knots is called a Solomon Bar. The Half Knots are worked on double cords as in the illustration.

No. 27. The Cowboy trick of tying an Overhand Knot with one hand. Weight the end of a 6-foot length of line and hold it in the right hand 5 feet from the ground in much the same manner as one would hold a pen, letting the end trail over the back of the hand and wrist. Form a six-inch long loop with the weighted end and hold it against the palm of the hand with the third and little fingers. With the index finger jerk the weight to hand level and manoeuvre the loop to scoop the weight. *A Left-Handed Overhand Knot* will result. The trick is not made easier by enlarging the loop. The smaller loop is more easily controlled.

No. 27.

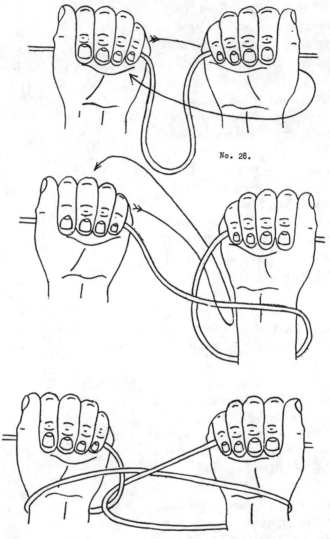

No. 28.

No. 28. *The Magic Overhand Knot.* Hold the ends of a 4-foot length of line in both fists. Pass the left fist completely round the right fist and return it to its original position. Then pass the left fist through the loop dangling from the right wrist in the manner indicated in the second illustration and draw both fists apart.

With a forward throwing movement shake the loop over the right fist; let go the end held in the left fist and clutch the loop. Draw the left fist along to the end of the line and reveal an Overhand Knot in the middle of the line. The loop is not difficult to clutch. It almost falls into the palm of the hand when the end is released.

This trick intrigued the 'Gully-gully' men in Port Said; and they are adepts at sleight of hand.

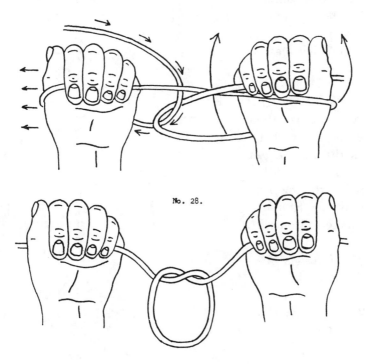

No. 28.

No. 29. *Magical Over-hand Knots.* Cast a number of Half Hitches on to the left thumb. Remove the Hitches from the thumb and pass the End of the cord through them from below. Say the magic word and draw out a number of Overhand Knots. If the knots are then opened up and the end re-entered the trick may be done in reverse.

No. 30. *The Thumb Knot* of the seamstress is either a Single or Double Overhand Knot. The thread is caught round the forefinger with a Single Hitch and the End rolled round the Standing Part. Sailmakers also use it.

No. 31. *A Single Over-hand* or *Thumb Knot.*

No. 32. *A Double Over-hand* or Thumb Knot.

No. 33. *Crown Sennit* is made with four strands worked with alternate Left and Right-Handed Half Knots.

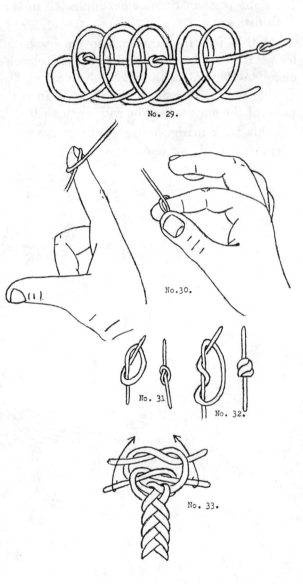

No. 29.

No.30.

No. 31

No. 32.

No. 33.

No. 34. *The Englishman's Loop* or *Angler's Knot.* Form an Open Loop with the Bight uppermost. Turn down the Bight to form two Loops. Draw the right Loop over the left and the left Loop under the right. Pass the Bight between the Ends and up through the Loops. Drawn taut this makes a handy Loop Knot. If opened out it will be seen to consist of two Overhand Knots.

No. 35. *West Country Whipping.* With a middled length of twine passed round the end of the rope to be whipped form a Half Knot on the upper side of the rope. Then form an identical Half Knot on the lower side of the rope, and continue on alternate sides until the required length is reached. Finish off with a Reef Knot.

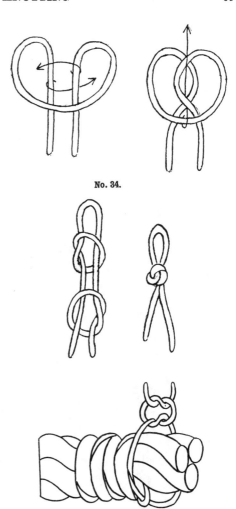

No. 34.

No. 35.

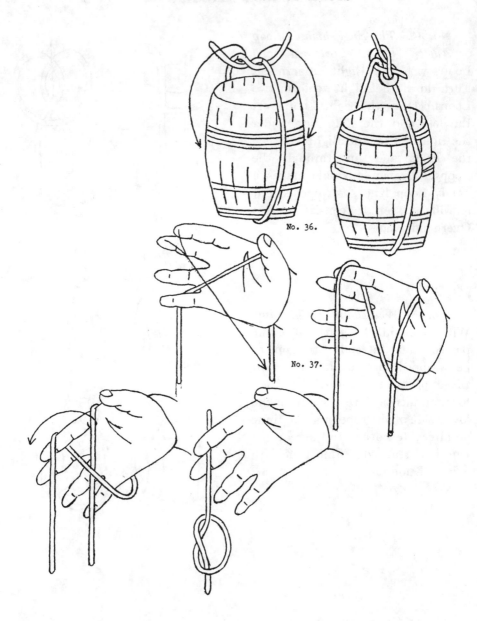

No. 36.

No. 37.

No. 36. Slinging a cask. Pass the middle of a length of rope under the cask and tie a Half Knot with the ends above the cask. Open the Half Knot and fit it round the bilge of the cask. In the illustration the ends have been bent together with a *Sheet Bend.*

No. 37. Another trick method of tying an Overhand Knot with one hand. Lay the cord across the extended palm of the right hand with one end round the little finger and the other end round the thumb and behind the wrist. With the first and second fingers nip the rear part of the cord and again extend the palm. Lower the palm allowing the Bight to drop over the nipped part of the cord. The result is a *Left-Handed Overhand Knot.*

CHAPTER XIII
THE FIGURE-EIGHT KNOT

The Figure-Eight Knot is well known and frequently used but has a less wide range than the Overhand Knot.

No. 38. Take hold of the Bight of an Open Loop and give it a half twist to the right. This forms a Single Turn. Pass the End behind the Standing Part and down through the loop of the Single Turn. This is the *Figure-Eight Knot.* Drawn up it acts as a temporary Stopper Knot.

No. 39. By taking an additional twist by passing and tucking the End a bulkier knot is formed.

No. 40. *A Slipped Figure-Eight Knot.* By slipping a knot it may be more easily untied. Instead of entering the End the knot has been completed by drawing the Bight through to form a loop.

No. 41. *A Chain of Figure-Eight Knots.* Arrange the cord as in the illustration and pass the end through the upper loops. As the cord is pulled through a chain of identical and equally-spaced Figure-Eight Knots will emerge.

No. 42. *Twist Braid or Bugle Cord.* Form a Figure-Eight Knot. Give the lower loop a half twist to the right and weave the End over and under. If the loop is lengthened the operation may be repeated as often as desired.

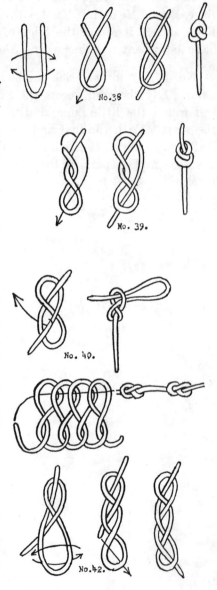

72

No. 43. *A Single-Strand Lanyard Knot* based on a Figure-Eight Knot.

No. 44. *A Two-Strand Lanyard Knot* made with two intertwined Figure-Eight Knots.

No. 45. Another example of a *Two-Strand Lanyard Knot* made with two intertwined Figure-Eight Knots.

No. 46. *The Single Bowline on the Bight.* Form a slipped Figure-Eight Knot (No. 40) and pass the End through the knot as indicated in the illustration.

No. 47. It is interesting to note that the basis of a *Simple Turk's Head* (Three Turns and two Bights) is the Figure-Eight Knot. Form a Figure-Eight Knot as in the first illustration. By passing a finger through it in the manner indicated the Turk's-Head is formed.

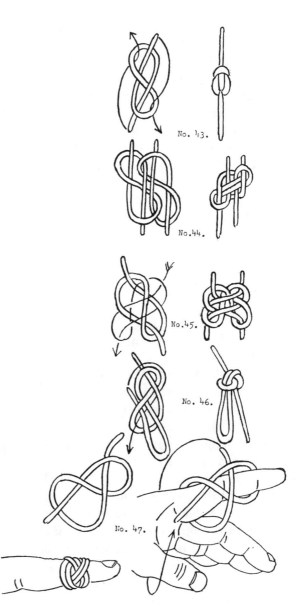

No. 43.

No. 44.

No. 45.

No. 46.

No. 47.

No. 48. The Figure-Eight Knot itself makes a decorative Turk's-Head. Draw a design on a piece of paper the exact circumference of the object to be decorated and attach this with rubber bands to the object. Take a suitable length of cord and follow the pattern passing it over and under where indicated. The cord may subsequently be doubled or trebled. Done with different coloured cords adds to the attractiveness.

No. 48

No. 49. The Cowboy trick of tying a Figure-Eight Knot with one hand. Weight the end of a 6-foot length of line and hold it five feet from the ground in much the same way as one would hold a pen, letting the end trail over the hand and wrist. Form a six-inch loop with the long end, give it a half twist to the right and hold it against the palm of the hand with the third and little fingers. With the index finger jerk the weight to hand level and manoeuvre the loop to scoop the weight. A Figure-Eight Knot will have been formed in the line. The trick is not made easier by enlarging the loop. The smaller loop is more easily controlled.

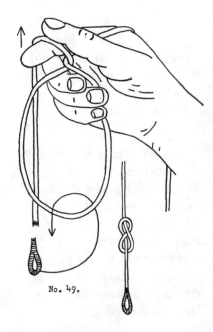

No. 49.

No. 50. *The Figure Eight Hitch,* used for attaching a fishline to a loop.

No. 50.

No. 51. The Figure-Eight Knot was employed in the medallions on this *Priest Cord.*

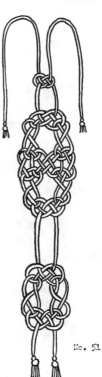

No. 51

CHAPTER XIV

THE SINGLE TURN AND THE HALF HITCH

The subject of this chapter is the most simple of all knotting forms, and as it is employed in thousands of knots only a limited number of examples covering a wide range of knots will be given.

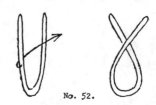

No. 52.

No. 52. When the End of an Open Loop is brought across the Standing Part a *Single Turn* is formed.

No. 53. A Hitch is a knot tied around or to some object. A *Half Hitch,* shown in the illustration, is tied with the End of a rope on its own Standing Part after it has been passed around an object.

No. 54. *Two Half Hitches.* This is commonly used for securing the end of a rope.

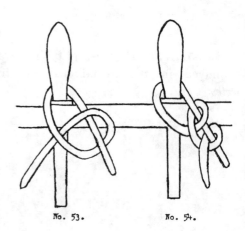

No. 53.   No. 54.

No. 55. *A Clove Hitch* consists of two identical Half Hitches. As it is not a particularly good Binding Knot the End is generally hitched to the Standing Part for added security.

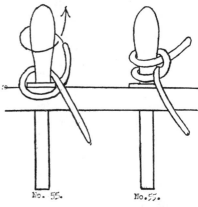

No. 55. No. 55.

No. 56. *The Cow Hitch* consists of two reversed Hitches. One of its uses is for the commencement of Netting.

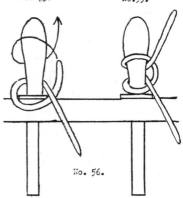

No. 56.

No. 57. *The Rolling Hitch.* One of its many uses is for stopping off a hawser when taking it from a winch or capstan to the bitts; another for securing a Handy Billy tackle to a stanchion.

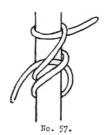

No. 57.

No. 58. *The Sheepshank.* Form three Single Turns, each one above the other. Draw the middle one through the two end ones. This looks more effective if done in one movement. The purpose of The Sheepshank is for shortening a rope without cutting it.

No. 59. *The Spanish Bowline.* An attractive knot which gives two Loops.

No. 60. *The Marlingspike Hitch.* Form a Hitch round an object. Draw the lower end out and pass it over the object. It is used with a marlingspike to get additional tension as when serving a wire splice.

No. 61. *A Turk's-Head of Four Turns and Three Bights* may be made from a Clove Hitch. Form a Clove Hitch and pass one end under and over through the loops and join it to the other end. Insert a finger at the point marked 'X' and the Turk's-Head will be made.

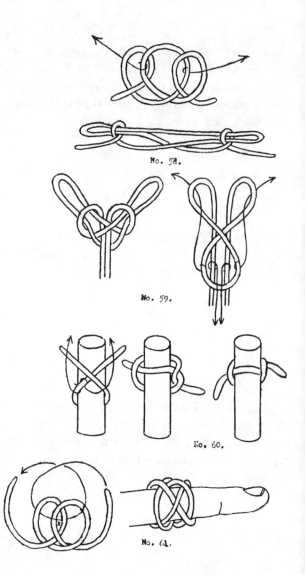

No. 58.

No. 59.

No. 60.

No. 61.

No. 62. *The Fisherman's Bend.* After the Round Turn is made the End is passed through it and then hitched to the Standing Part. Another Hitch may be added for greater security.

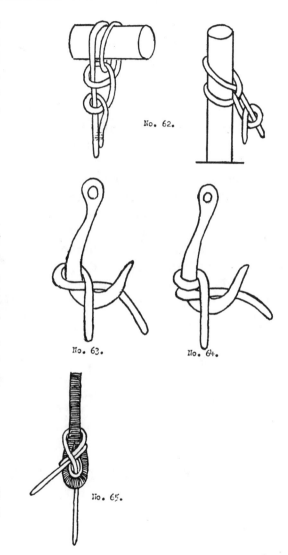

No. 62.

No. 63. *The Single Blackwall Hitch.* Here the Half Hitch has been solely, but effectively, employed. When the weight comes on the End it jams the Standing Part.

No. 64. *The Double Blackwall Hitch.* For greater security an additional Turn is taken round the hook.

No. 63.

No. 64.

No. 65. *A Double Becket Hitch.* Similar in construction to a Double Sheet Bend.

No. 65.

No. 66. *A Mat commenced with a Clove Hitch*. Form a Clove Hitch and follow the directions in the illustration with the Ends.

No. 67. *A Hitched Mat*. This Mat does full justice to the Half Hitch. The principle on which this Mat is made may be extended to any multiple of three. With twelve Half Hitches on the outer circle there would be six on the inner. The author made one as in the illustration measuring 21 inches in diameter and using $1\frac{1}{4}$-inch Point-line. The rope was threaded four times and took 125 feet.

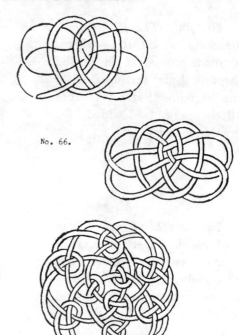

No. 66.

No. 67.

No. 68. A trick method of tying a *Clove Hitch* with one hand. Hang the cord over the right (or left) thumb. Hook the further end with the little finger. This forms a Half Hitch over the thumb. Twist the index finger round the remaining end to form the second Half Hitch. Bring the thumb and index finger together to form the Clove Hitch. This trick is even more effective if a Clove Hitch is tied with each hand at the same time.

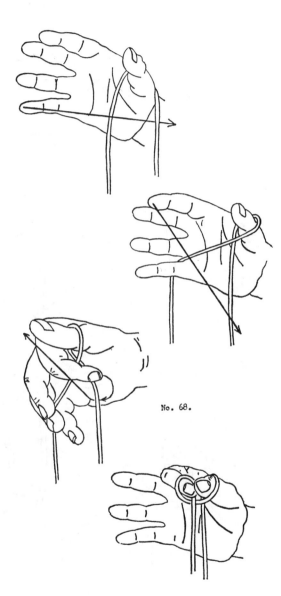

No. 68.

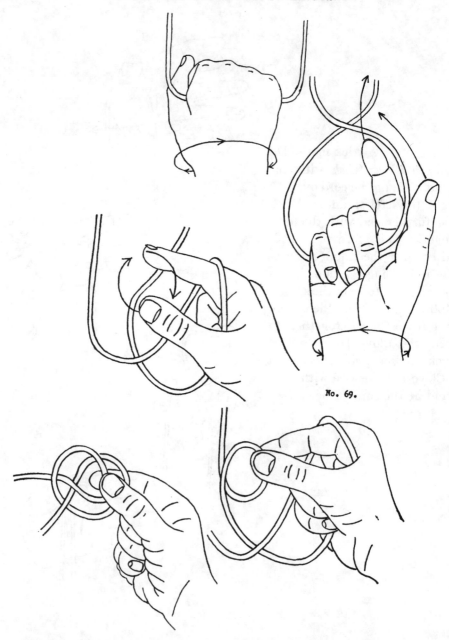

No. 69.

No. 69. *Picking a Clove Hitch off the Deck.* This is another trick method of tying a Clove Hitch with one hand. Arrange the cord in the form of an Open Loop on the deck. Grasp the Bight of the cord in the right hand. Turn the hand over to the right forming the first Half Hitch and open the first finger and thumb, but do not alter the position of the hand on the cord. Twist the hand to the left and place the finger and thumb over the part of the cord and in the manner indicated in the second and third illustrations. Give a sharp right twist to the cord with the finger and thumb to form the second Half Hitch. Bring the two hitches together to form the Clove Hitch. This trick can be done in a fraction of a second; much faster than the eye can follow.

No. 70. *The Sheet Bend.* This is the most commonly used bend aboard ship. Form an Open Loop with one rope. Pass the other rope behind and through the Open Loop, and make a Half Hitch with it round the Open Loop.

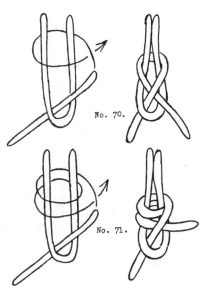

No. 70.

No. 71.

No. 71. *The Double Sheet Bend.* For greater security the Half Hitch is sometimes doubled round the Ends of the Open Loop.

CHAPTER XV

THE CARRICK BEND

The Carrick Bend is the most efficient way of uniting two ropes. It is also extensively employed in general knotting as the following examples show:

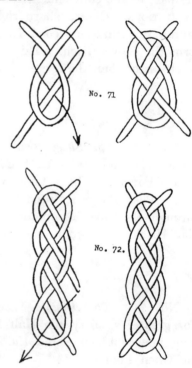

No. 71

No. 72.

No. 71. *The Carrick Bend.* Form a Single Turn by laying the End of one rope across its own Standing Part. Lay the End of the other rope under the Loop thus formed, and working in an anti-clockwise direction, pass the End over and under all parts.

No. 72. A Carrick Bend may be extended by drawing down the lower loop, giving it a half right twist, and Basket Weaving the two Ends. The knot may thus be extended as many times as required.

No. 73. *The Carrick Bend on the Bight.* Hang a cord over the left hand. Take the rear End and form a Single Turn over the thumb. Twist the Turn to the right and lay it across the part of the cord that lies across the palm of the hand. Take the left-hand one of the two Ends and pass it under the other End and upwards over and under. With a little practice this can be done in a matter of seconds.

No. 74. *The Sailor's Knife Lanyard Knot.* When the position has been reached as shown in No. 73, take each End in turn and pass it across the Standing Part on its own side and up through the centre of the Carrick Bend. Remove from the hand and draw the Ends and the Bight in opposite directions. Ease through the loose cord until the delightful knot is formed. This may then be doubled.

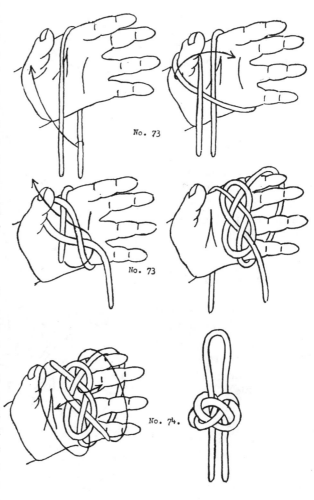

No. 73

No. 73

No. 74.

No. 75. *The Chinese Button Knot.* When the position has been reached as shown in No. 73, take each End in turn and pass it from its own side directly up through the centre of the Carrick Bend. Remove from the hand and grasp the two Ends in the fist. Draw the Ends into the fist until the pattern is formed shown in the illustration. Take in the slack and double the knot by paralleling the first lead with the two Ends.

No. 76. *The Carrick Bend Turk's Head.* When the position has been reached as shown in No. 73, pass the lower End through the lower part of the Standing Part; remove from the hand and lay flat on the table. Place the first finger and thumb in the upper and lower compartments of the Carrick Bend and squeeze the two loops together. Insert the finger through the loops and take in the slack. A Turk's-Head of Three Bights and Four Turns will have been formed.

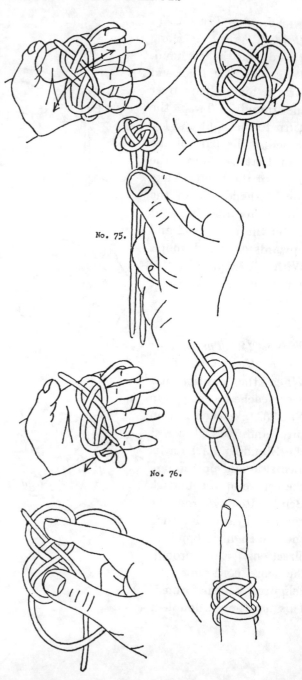

No. 75.

No. 76.

No. 77. *The Carrick Mat.* Form the Carrick Knot shown in the first illustration and double it by paralleling the first lead with an End.

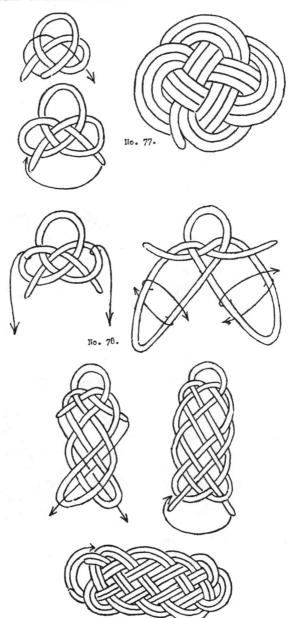

No. 77.

No. 78. *The Prolong Knot.* Form a Carrick Knot as shown in the first illustration. Extend the two lower loops, give them a half right twist and lay the right over the left. Basket Weave the two Ends. If the loops are made sufficiently long the process maybe repeated as often as required. The Mat may then be doubled by paralleling the first lead. The Ends should be stitched in place, preferably on the underside.

No. 78.

No. 79. *A Wide Carrick Mat.* Form a Carrick Mat and extend the upper loop. Reverse the right-hand End back through the knot parallel with itself. Form a right Single Turn in the long loop and pass it under and over between the parallels just formed. Finally weave the left-hand End through the space last formed. This makes an ideal Lanyard Knot

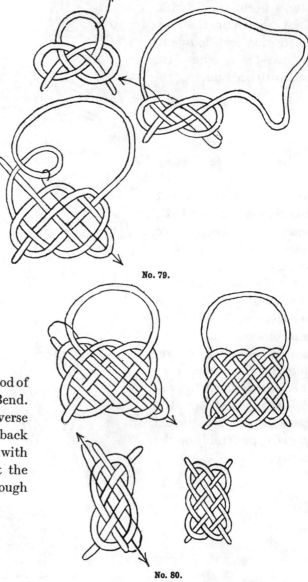

No. 79.

No. 80. Another method of enlarging a Carrick Bend. Form a Carrick Bend. Reverse the End at one corner back through the knot parallel with itself. Weave the End at the opposite corner back through the parallels just formed.

No. 80.

No. 81.   The Carrick Bend
was invariably used in the
making of ceremonial *Chinese
Priest Cords.*

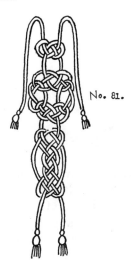

No. 81.

SECTION III

CHAPTER XVI

BASKET MAKING

If the reader is a sailor and he has made bellropes for his ship's bells, Coachwhipped the companion rails and accommodation-ladder stanchions; worked decorative Stopper Knots in the ends of manropes; graced the head of the gangway with an Oval or Ocean Plat Mat, and fitted a Paunch Mat to the Sea Boat then he might like to turn his attention to less important, but just as absorbing, knotting: ditty-bag lanyards, book marks, napkin rings, table mats, and baskets.

Sailors have always made baskets, but their construction, although made with a needle, was a form of crocheting. The form described in this Chapter, which the writer has developed, gives more scope for the production of fanciful designs.

A large bagging needle and a pair of scissors are the only instruments required. In addition a reel of stout cord or fishline; several sheets of typewriter copying paper, several sheets of carbon paper, and a large reel of adhesive tape. A 'mould' on which to build up the basket may be borrowed from the galley or kitchen.

The principle of this form of basket-making is the uniting of a number of Flat or Two-dimensional Knots of different design.

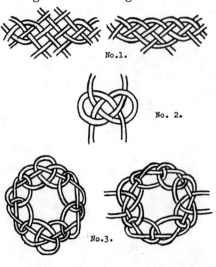

No. 1. *The Rim Design.* The left-hand design was modified as shown in the second illustration to form the upper and lower rims.

No. 2. *The Carrick Bend.* The cords descending from the rim are formed into Carrick Bends.

No. 3. *A Chinese Knot Design.* From the Carrick Bends one cord leads to the right and another to the left to form Chinese Knots. The design was slightly modified as shown in the right-hand illustration.

90

No. 4. *A Chinese Knot Design.* Also from the Carrick Bends two other cords lead down to form another design of Chinese Knot. This design was also slightly modified as shown in the right-hand illustration. The cords from these eight knots unite to form the lower set of Carrick Bends and are led from thence to the lower rim.

No. 5. *The Base of the Basket.* From the lower rim the cords continue to form the base of the basket. The design for this is shown on the left, and the modification in the right-hand illustration.

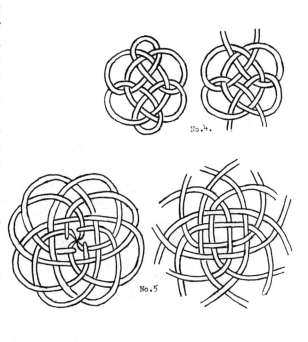

No. 6. The Detail of the Base. The illustration shows the connections between the base, the lower rim platting, and the lower Carrick Bends.

Procedure for Putting the Guide Lines on the Basin:—Divide the basin into eight equal parts and pencil lines along these divisions from top to bottom on the outside of the basin. Measure a close approximation of the size of the various designs. With the tracing paper and carbon paper make sixteen copies of the rim design (No. 1) and attach one of these over each of the pencilled divisions along the upper rim of the basin. It may then be necessary to add additional pieces of paper between these to complete the joining of the platting. See that the platted parts join accurately.

Make sixteen copies of the Carrick Bend (No. 2).

Make eight copies each of the two Chinese Knots (Nos. 3 and 4.)   Attach all of these designs to the basin in their respective positions with adhesive tape.

Now attach the other eight rim designs to the lower rim.

Make a copy of the Base Design (No. 5) and attach it to the bottom of the basin seeing that all leads join those from the lower rim correctly.   The detail of this is shown in illustration No. 6.

No. 6.

Before the actual weaving can be commenced it is necessary to cover the design with adhesive tape reversed, that is with the sticky side uppermost so that the cord may be stuck to it, as it is not possible to use pins for this purpose.   Cover only a section of the work at a time; and start with the upper rim.

Procedure for Weaving the Cord:—Prepare sixteen sets of cord each six feet in length. Take one of these cords, thread it through the needle, middle it, and commencing at the connection between the upper rim platting and any Carrick Bend stick the cord to the rim pattern following the guide lines and going over and under where indicated. When this first cord emerges at another Carrick Bend commence the second cord, immediately adjacent to it. Continue until eight cords have been used. Then with the remaining eight cords double the work just completed.

Having doubled the upper rim platting form the upper set of Carrick Bends with the doubled cord. It will be found easier to do this with single cords first, threading the others after.

With the upper of the two cords that emerge from the Carrick Bends form the adjacent Chinese Knots both on the right and left sides; and with the remaining cords form the lower set of Chinese Knots. Carry on with the lower set of Carrick Bends, the lower rim pattern, and the base pattern.

Having completed the base pattern double the cord back through the work until the already doubled work of the upper Carrick Bends is met.

Remove the adhesive tape and give the outside of the work a coat of shellac. When this is dry remove the basin and give another coat of shellac to the work inside and out. ,When dry cut short the excess cord and give the work a coat of flat white paint.

No. 6. The completed basket on the basin. For the sake of clarity the cord is shown doubled only as far as the Carrick Bends.

No. 7. To stiffen the upper rim of the basket and to form a ledge on which to rest the cover work a length of Single-strand Star Knot Sennit, the exact circumference of the inner rim, and sew it in position along the centre of the platting.

The illustration shows the sequence for the making of Single-strand Star Knot Sennit. Work each sequence taut as it is made, finally joining the two ends where the pencil is inserted.

No. 8. A circlet of Single-strand Star Knot Sennit.

No. 6.

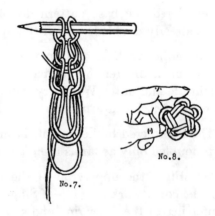

No. 7.

No. 8.

No. 9. The design for the Cover is the Half Hitched Mat. Measure the circumference of the inner rim and increase this by an inch, as the work tends to draw together with the second and third ply.

Draw a design similar to the illustration and stick it to a rounded surface: the surface of a medicine-ball was used by the author. Cover the design completely with reversed adhesive tape, that is with the sticky surface uppermost. Middle a long length of cord and thread it through the needle; then commencing at the centre stick the cord over the design following the guide lines going over and under where indicated.

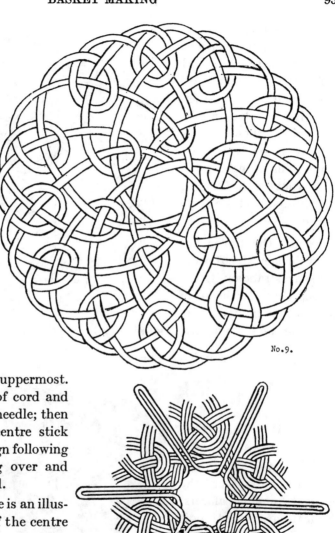

No.9.

No. 10. The figure is an illustration of a portion of the centre of the Cover. Its purpose is to demonstrate how the strands are prepared that are used to form the Star Knot handle on the Cover. As the cord passes the centre on

No.10.

each its curves for the third time a bight a foot long is made with the cord before it resumes its weaving. These bights are then cut, giving twelve strands. With six of these strands a Star Knot is formed. For details of making the Star Knot see the Chapter on Multi-strand Bellrope Knots.

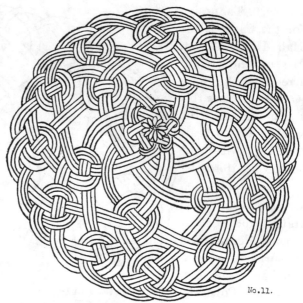

No.11.

When the Cover has been shellacked, cut short the spare strands and loose ends. Give it a coat of flat white paint before applying the gloss paint. Colours may be applied as one fancies.

No. 11.   The completed Cover.

No. 12. The completed Basket.

This work is the author's entry for the current Annual Seafarers' Education Service Handicraft Competition.

No. 12.

SECTION IV

CHAPTER XVII

MISCELLANEOUS KNOTS

In addition to the instructions given in Chapter **VI** for the raising of single-cord Square Turk's-Heads the novel method explained here makes the tying of these complicated knots simplicity itself.

No. 1. Part of the Bellrope, or other object, on which the knot is to be tied.

No. 2. Slip on two rubber bands.

No. 3. Tuck one end of the cord under the upper band. Take the cord at an angle of 45°, downwards, working from left to right, to the opposite side of the Bellrope.

No. 4. Tuck the bight of the cord under the lower band and take the cord at an angle of 45° upwards to the starting point.

No. 5. Pass the cord over, and tuck the bight under the band. Continue to lay the cord parallel and ahead of the last turn and with contrary over-and-under. A complete knot will be formed after three circuits with the cord. This will be a Turk's-Head of 3 Turns and 2 Bights (No. 6). Each subsequent completion of two circuits of the cord produces a raised Turk's-Head.

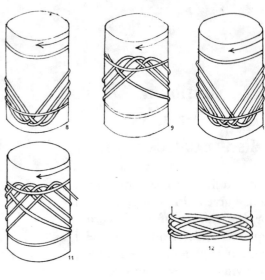

No. 12. A Square Turk's-Head of 5 Turns and 4 Bights.

No. 17. A Square Turk's-Head of 7 Turns and 6 Bights.

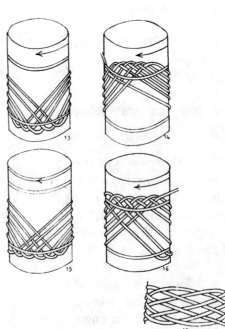

No. 22. A Square Turk's-Head of 9 Turns and 8 Bights. With this method, which may be mastered in a minute, there is no limit to the complexity of the knots that may be tied.

A Method of Tying Turk's-Heads Using Stretch or Crepe Paper. This method. which has been developed by the author, introduces an entirely new concept into the tying of Single-cord Turk's-Heads inasmuch as a pattern is enabled exactly to encircle the object:

No. 23. Draw the pattern on a piece of crepe paper. The pattern used in the illustration is a Square Turk's-Head of 9 Turns and 8 Bights.

No. 24. Attach the left side of the pattern to the object with adhesive tape.

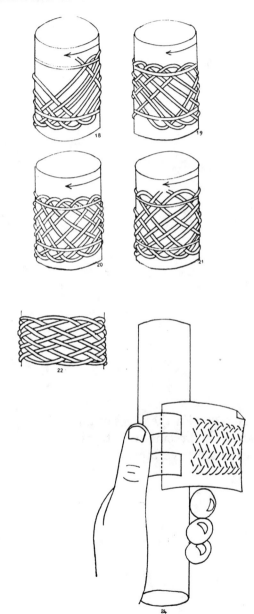

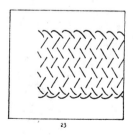

No. 25. Stretch the crepe
paper.

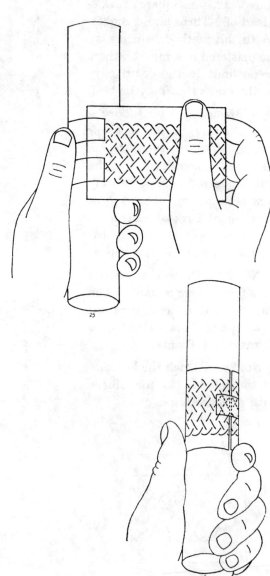

No. 26. Fit the edges of the
pattern and secure with trans-
parent adhesive tape.

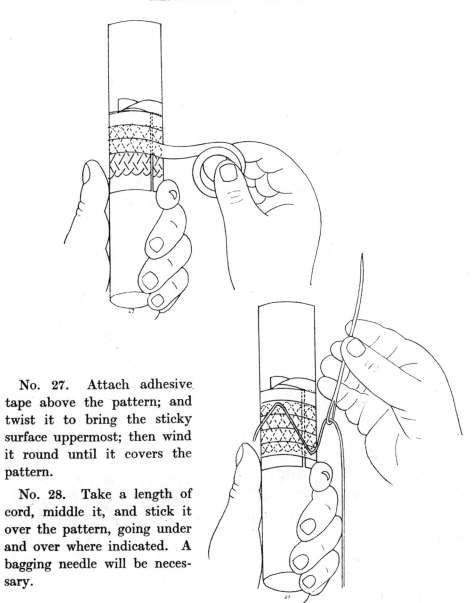

No. 27. Attach adhesive tape above the pattern; and twist it to bring the sticky surface uppermost; then wind it round until it covers the pattern.

No. 28. Take a length of cord, middle it, and stick it over the pattern, going under and over where indicated. A bagging needle will be necessary.

No. 29. After following the first lead twice a handsome Turk's-Head will result. Several patterns follow:

Nos. 30 and 31. A Square Turk's-Head of 11 Turns and 10 Bights.

No. 32. A Narrow Turk's-Head of 15 Divisions and 4 Diagonals.

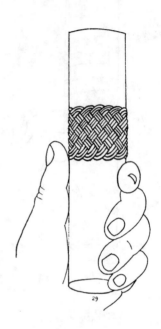

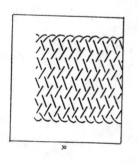

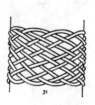

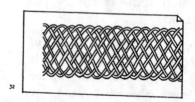

Nos. 33 and 34. A Long
Turk's-Head of 31 Turns and
12 Bights.

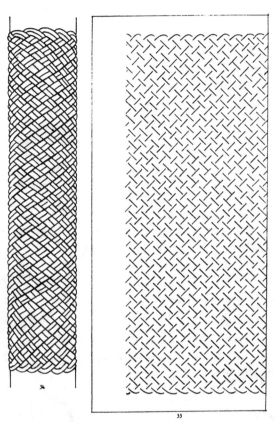

No. 35. A United Designs
Decorative Turk's-Head.

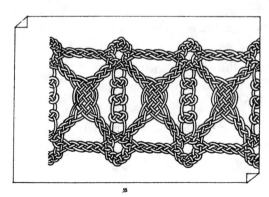

The Doubled Sailors' Knife Lanyard Knot. The Single Sailors' Knife Lanyard Knot is described in Chapter XV. No. 74. When doubled it makes an extremely handsome knot.

No. 36. Commence by forming two loops. This may be done over the palm of the hand and the thumb as described in Chapter XV, No. 74. Give the left hand loop a twist and place it over the standing part of the right-hand loop.

No. 37. Weave the cord under-and-over through the 2 loops to form a Carrick Bend on the bight.

No. 38. Taking each end separately, double the first lead and bring the ends up through the centre.

No. 39. Draw the two ends and the bight in opposite directions and work the slack through.

No. 40. The completed knot.

The Tack Knot. This is a seamanlike and decorative rope end knot.

No. 41. Unlay the rope end and with the three strands, tie a Single Wall Knot (Chapter II, No. 7).

No. 42. Above the Wall tie a Single Crown Knot (Chapter II, No. 8).

No. 43. Double the Wall by following the first lead.

No. 44. Double the Crown.

No. 45. Stick the strands down through the knot; taper the strands and serve them to the standing part of the rope.

No. 46. The completed knot.

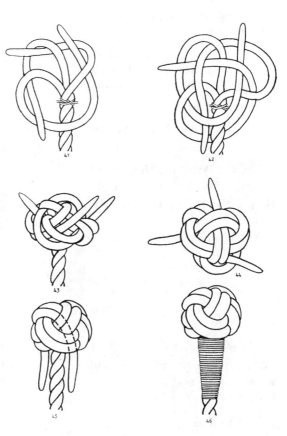

The Matthew Walker Knot. The multi-strand Matthew Walker Knot is described in Chapter IV, No. 14. The very useful 3-strand stopper knot is described here.

No. 47. Unlay the three strands and tie a Wall Knot (Chapter II, No. 7) with the left-hand strand.

No. 48. Wall the centre strand.

No. 49. Wall the right-hand strand. Work out the slack. Re-lay the rope and whip the end.

No. 50. The completed knot.

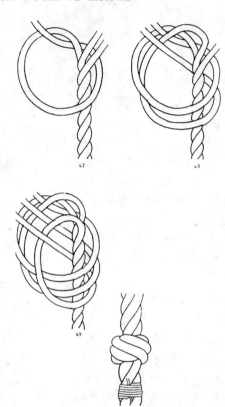

The Heaving-Line Knot. This knot is used by sailors to add weight to the end of a heaving-line.

Nos. 51 and 52. The number of turns taken is optional.

No. 53. The completed knot.

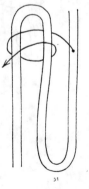

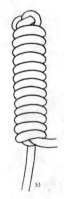

The Monkey's Fist. This knot is also used by sailors to weight the end of a heaving-line.

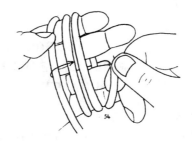

No. 54. Take three turns with the end of the line over the right-hand fingers.

No. 55. Take three more turns around the first three turns.

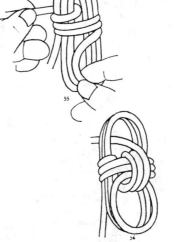

No. 56. Take three turns around the second turns and inside the first three turns. Work out the slack. The end is either seized or spliced to the standing part.

No. 57. The completed knot.

The Single-cord Star Knot Turk's-Head. Further instructions are given here of this attractive knot which is described in Chapter V, No. 39.

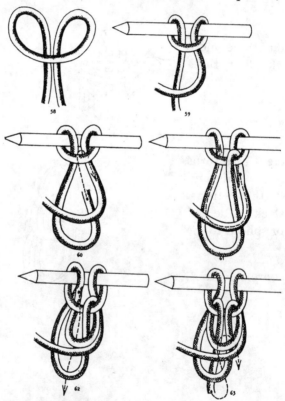

Commence with a Cow Hitch over a pencil (Nos. 58 and 59). Follow the sequence with the working end of the cord as depicted in Nos. 60 to 63. When a sufficient number of 'points' have been worked (No. 64) encircle the object

and reeve the cord through the
Cow Hitch (No. 65) and remove
the pencil. Complete the knot
by doubling the remaining work
(Nos. 66 to 68). No. 69 shows
the knot in plan. No. 70 shows
the completed knot.

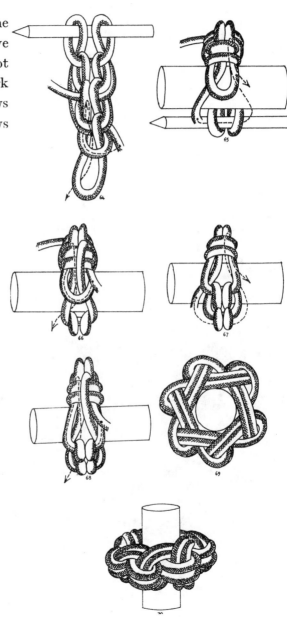

INDEX

INDEX

The number of an index item refers to the page on which the description appears.

113